KU-111-730

History
of
Angkor

© **KAILASH EDITIONS - 1997**
ISBN 2-84268-019-7

69, rue Saint Jacques - 75005 Paris - France
169, Lal Bahadur street - 605 001 - Pondicherry - India

Crédit photos : Jacqueline et Guy Nafilyan

MADELEINE GITEAU

History
of
Angkor

traduit du français par

Gail Armstrong

To the memory of Jean Boisselier

FOREWORD

Angkor was the most glorious capital of the Khmer kingdom and, although its history does not encompass all Cambodia, it does occupy a singular position in that country's chronology. We therefore intend to focus our attention on Angkor, to retrace its existence from its inception, at the end of the 9th century, to its decline during the 14th century, a decline which was followed by several centuries of dormancy.

No archives of Angkoran history exist; the oldest known chronicles were compiled at the end of the 18th century. A discovery of Angkor must therefore be undertaken through the study of its monuments. The inscriptions, sculpted on the stelae and on the piers of the sanctuary doors, were conceived as a means of sanctioning religious foundations and do not, therefore, take into account the profane aspects of life in Angkor.

Archeological study of the monuments completes the epigraphic data. The layout of the buildings inside the sanctuaries allows us to identify the organization of the cults as well as the roles which were bestowed on the priests. Moreover, the bas-reliefs offer documentary information comparable to that given by the epigraphic texts; they illustrate not only the gods and the myths, but also scenes of everyday life, of warfaring enterprises and of the organization of the palace.

It would therefore be impossible to bring Angkor's history to light without giving special attention to the study of the monuments, whose inscriptions and sculptures are the only true national witnesses to the past.

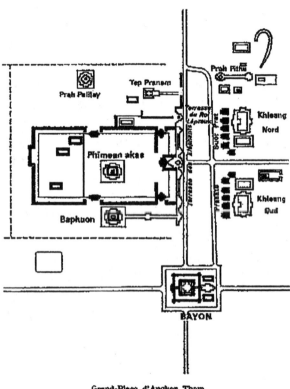

Grand-Place d'Angkor Thom

CHAPTER I

THE FOUNDING OF ANGKOR

1. Advent of Yashovarman I (889)

Crowned king of Cambodia in 889, Yashovarman reigned for a number of years before founding the capital city which would bear his name: Yashodharapura. In the same way that Rome was Urbs, the City, for the Latins, Yashodharapura became Angkor, the Capital, for the Cambodians. Yashodharavarman's reign began auspiciously. He succeeded his father, king Indravarman; his mother, Indradevi, having transmitted to him the dynastic rights of the two most ancient Cambodian kingdoms: Fu-Nan and Chen-La, as they are referred to in Chinese annals. The kingdom of Fu-Nan, founded in the southern part of the country, was a maritime nation; it's sovereignty was usurped in the 7th century by Chen-La, a land-based state which stretched across northern Cambodia and lower Laos, and whose religious centre was Wat Phu.

Upon his coming to power, Yashodharapura inherited a kingdom whose territories had recently been assembled and governed in an organized manner after having struggled with disparity for a hundred years. At the end of the 8th century, Jayavarman II (802-850) had undertaken the task of Cambodian independence and unification. He settled to the north of the Great Lake, in the alluvial plain, and his kingdom stretched out to the Mekong valley. He was crowned on Mount Mahendra, now called Phnom Kulen, he became known, in 802, as "absolute and only master of the land known as Shakravartin". Although he considered himself a Shakravartin, or universal ruler of his kingdom, Jayavarman II had to face princes who, after more than a century of dividing the Khmer nation, had become practically independent. It is certain that an important part of Cambodia remained outside of his control when he died in the capital city of Hariharalaya, fifteen kilometres from present day Siem Reap. It would be up to his two successors, his son Jayavarman III and especially Indravarman, a distant relation by marriage, to complete his work.

Indravarman managed to unify a large part of Cambodia under his rule; however, the principality of Bhavapura, in the northern part of the country, remained out of reach. Succeeding Jayavarman III, Indravarman resided in Hariharalaya. During his twelve-year reign, he transformed this town into a powerful city, erecting temples and digging an artificial lake, Indratataka. It is no doubt there that he oversaw the education of his heir, the future Yashovarman, by placing him under his own spiritual mentor.

As his "childhood without restrictions" passed by, nothing in

Yashovarman's education was left to chance. His mentor, Vamasiva, had gained his knowledge from a disciple of the Hindu philosopher Sankaracharya. Yashovarman remained a devotee of Shiva. His education was not restricted to philosophy. One inscription states that, "he practiced a wide range of gentle arts with zeal, as though he had learned and mastered them through affection and goodness." If we are to believe the inscriptions, the results obtained responded perfectly to the expectations set upon the young prince. He is portrayed as having a majestic beauty, capable of making the god of Love jealous; of being an untiring warrior, "his ardour destroyed the dangerous ardour of his enemies." Morally, he was "invested with these four qualities: energy, knowledge, virtue, method." It is even said that he possessed all of these emotional qualities because, "so given to goodness, he never passed in front of an unhappy person without stopping." With such a portrait in mind, it is not in the least surprising that his accession to the throne was met with great enthusiasm, "At his advent like (at sunrise) the lotuses raised their heads... the brilliance of the other stars was dimmed, the sun turned red on the horizon."

The correct behaviour of the sovereign constituted a guarantee of the kingdom's rightful order. Of necessity, the inscriptions stressed those qualities which must be found in the one who would make every effort to found the ideal capital of Cambodia, a veritable dwelling place for the gods on earth.

2. Foundation of the City

Upon his father's death, Yashovarman ascended to the throne in Hariharalaya. In the same way that Indravarman had consecrated the first foundation, the temple of Prah Ko, to the memory of this ancestors, Yashovarman erected, in 893, the four brick towers of

Lolei inside of which were displayed effigies of his parents and grandparents. Having thus accomplished his filial duties, he decided to abandon Hariharalaya in order to found a new capital.

At approximately twenty kilometres from Hariharalaya, the site of Angkor rises up on the plain which extends from the northern shore of the Great Lake at the edge of the sandstone plateau of Phnom Kulen. Three hills, or phnom, give shape to the region: the Phnom Bok, the Phnom Bakheng and the Phnom Krom. The two ancient capitals are situated close to two rivers, or stung; Hariharalaya is irrigated by the Stung Roluoh; near Angkor flows the Stung Siem Reap. The shores of the Great Lake are flooded during the rainy season as the waters of the Mekong flow out to the Tonlé Sap. The Stung Siem Reap has its source on the Phnom Kulen and flows into the Great Lake, not far from the Phnom Krom.

The banks of the Siem Reap river are highly fertile. It appears that, in the plain of Angkor as in that of Roluoh, the initial cultivation was of mountain rice; it was later replaced by irrigated rice fields, due to the evolution of hydraulic irrigation techniques. Traces of ancient occupations in the field are numerous, particularly in the regions to the west and to the south of Angkor. Among these still existent vestiges we find the temple of Ak Yom which may be associated with an urban centre, and which was abandoned in the 11th century when it was covered over by an artificial lake, the western baray. This lost city may have been a residence of Jayavarman II. To the east of Angkor stands the small temple of Kutisvara, evoking what may be the remains of a large property which this same king gave to his chaplain. The attribution of property to a high dignitary implies the bestowing of significance on the surrounding countryside. It is thus, in an already cultivated and populated land, that Yashovarman decided to found his capital.

In the eyes of the king and his councilors, the Angkor region presented a characteristic which rendered it unique: the Bakheng hill. The city must of necessity possess a sacred mountain. According to Indian tradition, the axis of the world is Mount Meru, dwelling place of the gods. Shiva, too, rules from a mountain top, that of the Kailasa. It is on the Phnom Kulen that Jayavarman II was crowned.

Yashovarman chose the Phnom Bakheng over the Phnom Bok and the Phnom Krom because it was lower and of lesser breadth, and could thus be more easily integrated into the city. Moreover, the Phnom Bok is too far from the Great Lake, whereas the Phnom Krom is too close, given that the floodwaters spill over into the neighbouring countryside. The Phnom Bakheng is much better situated, close to the lake but outside the flood zone, as well as being at a short distance from the Siem Reap river which could bathe the city's ramparts. The city was therefore well supplied with water without being in danger of the overflow from the Great Lake, in addition to which irrigation was possible and an inexhaustible reserve of fish was available.

It may appear that Yashovarman abandoned

Hariharalaya only to settle twenty kilometres further away. However, in Hariharalaya any new edifices had to be inserted into an already established framework. The young king no doubt desired not only a capital all his own, but also a city which could constitute the country's religious centre. The kingdom, the capital, hence the sovereign's dwelling place, must correspond to the home of the gods in the universe. To create a divine world at the heart of a nation was to assure the kingdom's prosperity. Angkor's geographical situation offered favourable conditions for its defense as well as its economy. It would be a mistake, however, to believe that Yashovarman chose this site only because the Phnom Bakheng rose up as a sort of Acropolis, because the Stung Siem Reap made irrigation possible, and because the Great Lake provided an inexhaustible source of fish. Such an interpretation implies the application of modern concepts onto a time when no such concepts existed. All the elements necessary for the creation of a microcosm were present: on the Phnom Kulen the river flowed onto the saintly images sculpted in sandstone in its bed, onto the linga, Shiva's phallic symbol. These waters which were sanctified through contact with the divine brought much more than merely the soil's fertility, they guaranteed the capital's and, thus, the entire kingdom's felicity. It was far more important to erect a temple on the Phnom Bakheng than a fortress.

The inscription in Sdok Kak Thom, which tells of the founding of Angkor, states that, "the king erected the

Central Mountain" and that his spiritual master, the brahmin Vamasiva, "erected the sacred linga in the middle". In displacing the capital, Yashovarman's goal was not simply to obtain the glory of attaching his name to the creation of a city; his desire was to establish a sacred residence whose symbolism would establish a divine dwelling place on earth, and which would shine upon the entire kingdom. While there may have been an element of pride involved, to reduce it to a mere manifestation of a potentate's desire for glorification would be to denigrate the fundamentally religious aspect of his act.

3. Yashovarman's city

The city founded by Yashovarman was not the Angkor Thom adorned with monumental doorways which we now so admire. As was stated, its centre was the Phnom Bakheng which rises to the south of Angkor Thom's moat. Thus the city shifted gradually between the last years of the 9th century and the end of the 12th. In actual fact, Angkor was rebuilt some three hundred years after its foundation. The first searchers thought that Angkor Thom, which had kept the name of Yashodharapura, corresponded to Yashovarman's city, a false identification which led to errors in the establishment of the monuments' chronology.

Yashovarman's capital was not bound by walls, its ramparts consisted of a double earthen enclosure. It is even possible that they did not completely encircle the city. Only the southern part of this quadrilateral is relatively well preserved. A moat ran the length of the enclosures; but, to the east, it is likely that the Siem Reap was diverted so that it ran along-side the earthen ramparts. It is still possible to see a part of the enclosures, especially from a south-eastern angle. The ancient moats produced sufficient moisture to allow for their conversion into rice fields by the peasants.

4. The Phnom Bakheng

We do not know how this city was organized. Only the edifices of a religious nature were built of masonry; the buildings made of perishable materials have long since disappeared. Furthermore, the entire northern part of the first capital was covered over by Angkor Thom. From the first city of Angkor only the temple on the Phnom Bakheng may be indisputably attributed to Yashovarman's reign. In the inscriptions of Sdok Kak Thom, the Phnom Bakheng is designated as being the Central Mountain. It is a hill measuring approximately sixty metres in height, which dominates the whole of Angkor's site. The temple was built on its summit.

Crowning the hill, the temple's five principal sanctuaries are staggered on a 13-metre high pyramidal terrace boasting five grades. The central, and most important, sanctuary was raised above the other four corner edifices. The overall plan is centred around this one sanctuary. One may gain access to the terrace's summit by stairs which mount the axes. The terrace and all the buildings which it supports are made of sandstone. The base of the pyramid is surrounded by forty four brick sanctuaries. In Indravarman's time, a high pyramid had already been erected in Hariharalaya, at the temple of Bakhong. The layout consisting of five sanctuaries at the peak of the pyramid was new, however, and so rich in symbolism that it would be reproduced for centuries to come. Apart from the sanctuaries at the summit and the base, the Phnom Bakheng temple sports sixty smaller temples built on the pyramid's grades, on the either side of the stairways' angles.

J. Filliozat asserts that the quantity and the layout of the sanctuaries of this mountain temple are not without meaning. The sanctuaries total 108, a significant number, as are all those containing 1 and 8. There are 10,800 stanzas in the Veda; in the Indian calendar, each day is divided into 30 periods, the muhurta, and a years of 360 days contains 10,800 muhurta. Finally, if we multiply the number 27, which represents the lunar mansions, by the number 4, which corresponds with the number of lunar phases, the outcome is 108.[1]

The sanctuaries' layout is as significant as their number. It has long since been noted that the five staggered sanctuaries reflect the five summits of Mount Meru, home of the gods. Thirty three gods reside on Mount Meru. J. Filliozat remarks that, on the Phnom Bakheng, when one contemplates each face of pyramid, one perceives only three sanctuary towers, all the others remaining hidden from view. Each of these sanctuaries contains a linga, thus each god is represented by a linga, since all is Shiva.

At the summit, only three towers are visible when loo-
king at one of the temple's faces; one tower rises above
the other two, reflecting the divine trinity dominated by
Shiva. The Phnom Bakheng is thus an authentic Mount
Meru, home of the gods and axis of the world.
The revered divinity of the Phnom Bakheng was
considered to be the essence of royalty. The text of the
inscriptions of Skok Kak Thom recalls that the king's spiritual leader, the brahmin Vamasiva, "erected a linga on
Mount Sri Yassodharagiri whose beauty was equal to that
of the king of the mountains (Himalaya)". The Khmer
text of the same inscription states that Yashovarman,
designated under his posthumous name of
Paramasivaloka,

"established the royal city of Sri Yashodharapura and brought the
Kamarateng jagat ta raja from Hariharalaya to this city. Thus HRH
Paramasivaloka erected the Central Mountain. The lord of Sivasrama
(Vamasiva) founded a Sacred Linga in the centre."

Nothing in the inscription allows us to specify what
the "Kamarateng jagat ta raja" was. It was thought that
this Khmer expression was the equivalent of devaraja,
which was translated as "god-king", and it was believed
that this god-king could have been a idol personifying
the royal essence. The term devaraja appears in the text
concerning Jayavarman II. The problem is, in fact, far
more complex. J. Filliozat noted that kamrateng jagat corresponded with jagadisvara, "god of the world", which
designates Shiva as king, according to a well-established
south Indian tradition. It is not the essence of royalty but

rather Shiva who was ritually established in Yashodharapura. The linga erected in the central sanctuary by Vamasiva bears the name Yassodharesvar, "lord of Yashodhara", the manifestation of Shiva who is the "lord of Yashovarman".

A sacred zone, the sivakshetra, must be built around the linga and must contain trees where the ascetics can meditate. The circumference of a shivakshetra may measure up to 60 cubits. The outer enclosure of Phnom Bakheng, measuring 650 by 440 metres, attains proportions which are only slightly inferior to those of a sivakshetra.

The capital was thus an especially sacred site, a veritable microcosm at the centre of which resided the king's god of predilection. How was this site consecrated? What ceremonies took place there? There are no indications. The author of the inscriptions of Sdok Kak Thom does not belabour the point; the goal of this text was to relate the merits of a sacerdotal family, and not to recount the kingdom's history. It was only in order to situate events which affected this lineage that the engraver inserted a handful of the sovereign's deeds.

Within the walls of the first Angkor, the Phnom Bakheng temple is the only monument which, to our knowledge, was indisputably erected by Yashovarman. No vestiges of a palace or abode dating back to this era have been found to date. The ornamental sculptures of the temples scarcely reflect any one particular style of architecture. It is therefore difficult to imagine Yashovarman's capital other than hypothetically.

5. The city's outskirts

Yashodharapura was not isolated in a desert plain. A road was built which linked it to Hariharalaya. The road began at the southern entrance to the new capital, and ended at the north-east corner of Indratataka. Villages which no doubt depended on a handful of large estates sprung up in the region. Small sanctuaries, such as Prasat Patri, which are similar in style to Bakheng, and which were probably the site of rural cults, are still present in the area to the south of the ancient walls.

It may be postulated that a number of villages were established in the region between the Great Lake and the edge of the Phnom Khulen plateau. It is only through examination of the placement of religious vestiges that we can prove the existence of a population on this plain. A hermitage may be isolated in the bush, but a temple is generally close to an urban centre, or at least to a village. Three towers consecrating the Trinity, Shiva, Vishnu and Brahma, crown the Phnom Krom and the Phnom Bok.

Considerable hydraulic works were undertaken to the east of the city. The king ordered an immense waterway, the Yassodharatataka, which is now known as the Eastern baray. A dyke measuring 7 km in length by 1.8 km in width retained the water in this artificial pond. Four stelae, placed at the corners of the dyke, reinforced the religious significance of this immense basin. In order to complete the management of the waterways, the Siem Reap was diverted and linked to the city's moats.

6. The monasteries

We do not know how Yashodharapura was organized, nor how the inhabitants of the capital or the villages lived. We do, however, have fairly precise information regarding life in the monasteries which were founded by Yashovarman, near the Eastern baray. The king erected monasteries to the south of Yassodharatataka. The inscriptions sanctioned the foundation of these establishments. In the first, Brahmanasrama, dwelled the monks of Shaivist sects; in the second, the Vaishnavasram, were the Vishnuists. The stelae of the foundations were discovered in the places where these monasteries had been established. A third stele was found in Angkor Thom, near Tep Pranam; it commemorates the foundation of a Buddhist ashram. This stele was displaced, however, and it is thus possible that the third monastery was also built on the dyke to the south of the baray. On both the faces of these stelae, the same text is inscribed in different characters. On one side we find characters which may be traced back to northern India. The inscriptions give extremely precious indications regarding the organization of the monasteries, as well as their means of subsistence. They speak of living cells, classrooms and libraries.

Each monastery is run by a Superior who must assure "this hermitage's abundant wealth". One of his essential tasks is teaching; there is mention of the residence of masters and students who must receive staples of subsistence: four toothpicks, eight areca nuts, a portion of husked rice, sixty betel leaves, as well as a faggot of wood, which must be given to the masters and the students who are bachelors. Some instruments are also put at the students' disposal. Certain items are among those placed in the cells: "bedding, razors and scissors will be replaced every year in each cell". Other objects are distributed according to merit: "the virtuous student will receive virgin leaves, animal coal, chalk". The virgin leaves were perhaps lantana leaves which were prepared for writing.

The students and the masters who lived in the monastery enjoyed a privileged status. It is clearly stated that the one who instructs is more revered than the one who does not communicate his knowledge. However, the monastery was open to various categories of the disaffected and could be used by those seeking asylum. Moreover, it was expected that honoured guests were to be received, and the respect they were to be shown was clearly indicated. It is added:

"and if the King were to come here with his wives, he (the Superior) will take care to honour him as a god, according to the hermitage's resources as, being supreme master on Earth, he is revered as the guru of the world."

In addition, the king's daughter, his granddaughters or his old wives were to be honoured as were the other guests, although it is specified that, "they will not show themselves in the cells". Finally, as concerns women, "whose vanity is well known, they will not be allowed to enter here". The interest of these inscriptions extends beyond monastic life; we may therein discover the hierarchy of Angkoran society.

7. The value of Yashovarman's works

It is without a doubt that the foundation of Angkor was the greatest work of Yashovarman's twenty year reign[2]. It must be stated, however, that this sovereign also boasts military triumphs: inscriptions in which he is mentioned were found from lower Laos to the shores of the Gulf of Siam. He also undertook further construction far from Angkor. Unaware of the prestigious destiny which awaited Yashodharapura, the king had bestowed great significance on the city, namely that of a representation of the world and home to Shiva, in the centre of the kingdom. The rich symbolism of the capital was not of Yashovarman's invention; the idea is Indian in origin. The city possess a Central Mountain, the Phnom Bakheng, in the image of Mount Meru; an earthen enclosure, comparable to the cosmic mountain ranges, surrounds the city; the large artificial lake is at once a tirtha, or sacred basin, as well as a symbol of the ocean. Yashovarman's successors never lost sight of Angkor's profound significance: it was the ideal capital which guaranteed the kingdom's prosperity and invulnerability. The city will be somewhat displaced, although it will remain a divine dwelling place even after it has been abandoned by the monarchy.

1 The temple of Phnom Bakheng
(end 9th cent.), centre of the first city of Angkor,
aerial view.

2 Eastern face of Baksei Chamkrong
(first half 10th cent.).

3 Prasat Kravan, northern sanctuary,
lower bas-relief, (first half 10th cent.).

4 Prasat Pre Rup, royal temple
(2nd quarter 10th cent.)

5 Phimeanakas, temple of the royal palace
(2nd half 10th; early 11th cent.).

CHAPTER II

ANGKOR IN THE 10TH CENTURY

1. Angkor under Yashovarman's first successors

Ascended to the throne in 889, Yashovarman died some twenty years later. After his death, he was endowed with the posthumous name Paramasivaloka, a name by which, according to tradition, he will be designated in all inscriptions posterior to his reign. Heirs to the throne, his two sons reigned successively under the names Harshavarman I and Ishanavarman II. The first was no doubt still living in 922; the second may have passed away by 928.

We know very little of these two sovereigns. The inscription in Baksei Chamkrong sings the praises of Harshavarman by depicting him as being, "an agile fencer, shining with glory, disciplined in his meditation, eager to serve others, poised in his heroism". This text also celebrates, "his younger brother, born of the same mother, Sri Ishanavarman, victorious, more beautiful than Love, master of all arts".

In 921, the future Jayavarman IV, uncle to these two kings, left Yashodharapura in order to settle in Chok Gargyar, on the site of Koh Ker, situated approximately one hundred kilometres from Angkor. It was thought that this prince had attempted to usurp power and that, beginning in 921, there had been a scission in the kingdom with Jayavarman ruling in Koh Ker, whereas Yashodharapura remained the capital of Harshavarman and Ishanavarman. In the texts, however, Yashovarman is not depicted as a usurper. The inscription in Baksei Chamkrong states simply,

"the very talented Sri Jayavarman, impassioned by Sri, founded a city which by its magnitude was the seat of power for the Sri of the Three Worlds."

The stele at Sdok Kak Thom speaks clearly of the installation at Koh Ker and of the transfer to this residence of the Kamrateng jagat ta rajah, but does not specify the date. Another inscription places the advent of Jayavarman IV in 928. Whatever the case may be, Ishanavarman's death entailed a temporary desertion of Angkor.

During the eighteen years which followed Yashovarman's death, two important foundations were erected in Angkor, namely the temples of Baksei Chamkrong and Prasat Kravan. Raised to the north of Phnom Bakheng, near the foot of the hill, the Baksei Chamkrong sanctuary cannot be compared to Yashovarman's great temple. It was raised by Harshavarman I in homage to his father and mother. It consists of a sanctuary built on a high, graded base. It is an extremely refined construction; its proportions are particularly harmonious and, nowadays, the warm hues of the brick and laterite, which have been eroded over time, seem to shine out from amidst the trees in the forest. The inscriptions carved on the piers of the sanctuary doors tell us that, in this temple, Harshavarman had erected two gold effigies of Isvara, in other words Shiva and his wife Uma. Inscriptions date the Prasat Temple in 921. It consists of a group of five brick tower sanctuaries, or prasat. The central and northern prasat sport bas-reliefs sculpted in the brick of their inner walls. Few examples remain of sanctuaries with decorated interiors. Prasat Kravan may here be compared to a modern day temple in south-east Cambodia: Prasat Neang Khmau whose walls inner face bear traces of paintings which reveal the same iconography.

The foundation of Prasat Kravan was not the work of the reigning sovereign, but rather that of several high dignitaries. The greatest donations were made by a minister named Mahidharavarman. It was he who, in 943 saka (921 AD)[3], erected an image of Vishnu under the name of Trailokanatha, "Lord of the Three Worlds", in the central sanctuary. The reliefs which cover the walls of the cella represent Vishnu three times. The bas-relief of the southern wall no doubt depict this god taking the three steps toward the conquest of the Three Worlds, namely Earth, Intermediary Space and Sky.

The five sanctuaries of Prasat Kravan constitute an important foundation. The slaves offered by various donors for its upkeep were many, numbering perhaps more than two hundred and fifty. The foundation continued to be maintained over time. A brief inscription in the central sanctuary tells us that, in 971, a donor offered slaves to the god Trailokanatha.

At the same time, in Yashodharapura, king Harshavarman was erecting a sanctuary which appears modest in comparison to the edifices of the upper dignitaries, whose foundations stand as proof of the existence of a wealthy aristocracy. Although the royal foundation consists of a sanctuary elevated on a high, graded base, inside of which were installed a well and a small cell, the mandarin foundation is a group of prasat built on a simple, flat socle. The two temples apparently correspond to different religious orientations.

We do not know what became of Yashodharapura when, upon the death of Ishanavarman, the crown went to Jayavarman IV. The latter established his capital in Koh Ker, where he resided until 921. As for Yashodharapura, it no doubt suffered the same fate as Hariharalaya; it appears probable that, for approximately twenty years, it held the role of a provincial town.

2. The monarchy's return to Angkor (944)

Jayavarman IV died in Koh Ker in 1942, leaving the succession of power in the hands of his son, Harshavarman II. Two years later, this new king passed away. Whether accidental or not, the death of Harshavarman II put an end to Jayavarman IV's lineage. In 944, the crown was passed on to his nephew, Rajendravarman II, son of Yashovarman's older sister, Mahendradevi, who had married Mahendravarman, prince of Bhavapura. This latter's principality appears to have been located in northern Cambodia. Heir to

Bhavapura by his father and to Cambodia by his mother, Rajendravarman achieved the unification of the kingdom which had been the dream of all his predecessors, from Jayavarman II onward. The numerous inscriptions engraved under Rajendravarman's reign are ripe with praise. The inscription in Baksei Chamkrong boasts, "the charming beauty" of this king "of whom the world sung the nascent virtues".

Rajendravarman immediately returned the capital to Angkor, thus re-instituting the framework of the monarchy which had been established by his uncle Yashovarman. An inscriptions tells of how, "he restored the sacred city of Yashodharapura which had long remained empty."

An entourage of upper dignitaries settled in Angkor along with him. Among the king's councilors was the brahmin Sivacharya who had begun his career under Ishanavarman II. Another person, who is referred to only by his title of Rajakula Mahamantrin, must have had an especially political role. He must have survived Rajendravarman and have maintained his position under the following reign. Upon a third man, Kavindrarimathana, who was a Buddhist, the king bestowed the task of erecting several monuments, namely that of the Royal palace and the temple of Eastern Mebon. At the end of the reign enters the brahmin Yajnavaraha, an upper dignitary who was a relative of the royal family, and who was to play an important role in the future. These individuals enjoyed a number of privileges as well as providing the inspiration for many royal initiatives. The inscriptions in the sanctuaries tell of their wealth. Among the foundations of the upper dignitaries, the most renown is the temple erected by Yajnavaraha, in 967, on the site of Banteay Srei.

3. Angkor's royal foundations under Rajendravarman II (944-968)

By establishing foundations, Rajendravarman set a two-fold goal: one the one hand he hoped to affirm the legitimacy of his lineage; on the other hand, he wished to strengthen the ties which bound him to Yashovarman and the Angkoran monarchy.

In 947, in Baksei Chamkrong, in this temple which was erected at the beginning of the century by Harshavarman, "to increase his parents' dharma", the inscription states that Rajendravarman, "this competent king, gifted with divine vision, added this incomparable golden image of Parmesvara[4], with the appropriate rites and the splendour of this prasat decorated with stucco". It was wondered whether Rajendravarman constructed this sanctuary which, nowadays, crowns the upper base of Baksei Chamkrong, or whether he merely applied the stucco adornment. G. Coedès retained the first hypothesis. Since that time, J. Boisselier noted that the tower-sanctuary, the prasat, was from the same era as the base, and that the monument had merely been embellished with stucco; in covering the Baksei Chamkrong sanctuary, elevated on a graded pyramid, with stucco, Rajendravarman would have given it a splendour comparable to that of Kailasa; the Kailasa being the magnificent and unshakable home of Shiva and Uma whose images were therein erected by Harshavarman. The care which Rajendravarman gave to this foundation, at the beginning of the century, constituted a renewal of the traditions established by Yashovarman. Yashovarman's initial foundation had been the temple of Lolei, erected in homage to his predecessors, in the centre of Indratataka, the pond which had been built by Indravarman. The first construction ordered by Rajendravarman was the temple of Eastern Prasat Mebon, erected in homage to his ancestors in the centre of Yashodharatataka, the Eastern baray. Although the Eastern Mebon, like Lolei, forms an island in the middle of an artificial lake, the aspect of the two monuments is different. Lolei contains four towers built on the same base; the Eastern Mebon presents five staggered towers on a terrace. This layout evokes that of the summit of the Phnom Bakheng. The Phnom Bakheng is made of sandstone, however; the Prasat Mebon is made of brick, set upon a laterite base. Rajendravarman's reign marks a return to the use of stucco covered brick. The adornment was of stucco; only the window frames were sculpted in sandstone.

Two of Mebon's five towers were dedicated to the king's parents in the form of Shiva and Uma. The central and the other two corner sanctuaries contain representations of the Trinity; the central linga of Rajendresvara was superior to the four other images. In the centre of the Eastern baray, guarded at each corner by stone elephants, and adorned with stucco, Prasat Mebon must have been a monument of great beauty. The lines which remain are wonderfully harmonious: on the grades, long rooms stretch out horizontally, contrasting with the vertical thrust of the corner stairways and the sanctuaries at the summit.

Although it is not larger, the Pre Rup temple, founded in 961, is even more imposing than the Prasat Mebon. The pyramid which supports it measures more than twelve metres high; its summit is also crowned with five quincuncial prasat, according to a plan centred around the main sanctuary. In order to edify Pre Rup, laterite and stucco-covered brick were again used, as in Mebon. The two styles are closely linked although their composition and, more important still, their significance are divergent.

The temple of Pre Rup would replace neither the Phnom Bakheng nor the Prasat Thom of Koh Ker, in which were venerated, respectively, Yashodharesvara, the "Lord of Yashodhara" and Tribhuvanesvara, the "Lord of the Three Worlds". A new cult was organized in Pre Rup through the enthronement of the linga Rajendrabhadresvara; hence Bhadresvara the "Auspicious Lord" is the divinity of Wat Phu, the lingaparvata, holy site for the dynasty of current day Southern Laos.

One gained access to Pre Rup, built on solid ground, by a road bordered by stone markers. On the grades, the long rooms have much more importance than at Prasat Mebon and, on the eastern face, five towers were constructed at the base of the pyramid[5].

This temple, with the warm hues of its laterite base and the soft pink of its bricks, is one of the most magnificent works of Angkoran architecture. The frames of the windows and false doors, in a slightly green sandstone, were sculpted with utmost care. On the walls of certain sanctuaries, in the remnants of stucco which still cling to the brick, female divinities, slimmer and more elegant than those of Phnom Bakheng, have not abandoned their role of protectors.

Between 957 and 961, at the same time as he was constructing the great temples to the east of Yashodharapura, Rajendravarman undertook the edification of the Royal Palace.

It is here that we find the first state of Phimeanakas whose name evokes the "Celestial Palace" which was already being erected within the inner precinct of the Royal Palace.

The Phimeanakas had no gallery built on the grades of the laterite pyramid; in its composition, this pyramid closely resembles that of Pre Rup. From this era onward, the Royal Palace occupied the site which it would continue to occupy for as long as the kings resided in Angkor.

4. Foundations of the dignitaries under Rajendravarman

In the mid-10th century, the kings were not alone in erecting sanctuaries. Many important foundations were the works of upper dignitaries. Three temples were edified in the region of Angkor.

The first mandarin foundation, erected under this reign in the Angkor region, was the Buddhist temple of

Bat Chum. It was founded in 953 by Kavindrarimathan, the individual whom Rajendravarman had put in charge of the construction of the Palace and of Prasat Mebon. Despite the establishment of a Buddhist monastery by Yashovarman, it seems that Buddhism experienced somewhat of a decline during the 9th and early 10th centuries. An inscription dating back to the end of the 10th century speaks of a rebirth of Buddhism; it tells of the restoration of broken images and of the creation of monasteries. The three towers of the small temple of Bat Chum were to shelter an image of Buddha, and representations of the two divinities of Mahayana Buddhism[6].

The two other temples erected by the dignitaries are dated at the very end of the reign; both are Brahminic. One is the temple of Banteay Srei, among the most renown of the Angkor group. Founded in 967 by the brahmin Yajnavaraha, it was no doubt constructed under the following reign; the other sanctuary is that of Prasat Prah Enkosei which rises on the left bank of the Stung Siem Reap. Of this temple there remain two brick towers, erected in 968, the year of Rajendravarman's death, by a brahmin come from India, Divakarabhatta, who had married one of the king's daughters.

The upper dignitaries' foundations are of particular interest in the study of Angkor as they present, in juxtaposition with the royal architecture, monuments of a noticeably different type, in addition to which the inscriptions which they contain convey precious information regarding the social and legal organization of Cambodia at that time. They speak of the transmission of goods by donation or by heritage and, in this context, they expose familial genealogies.

5. End of Rajendravarman II's reign

Rajendravarman II died in 968, after a reign which was marked by a victory over the Chams. Having invaded Champa, the Khmers seized and brought back the golden statue from the Po Nagar temple in Nha Trang. Rajendravarman's death entailed a transfer of power to his son Jayavarman V who was no doubt a very young man at the time, perhaps even a child.

6. Advent of Jayavarman V

"Sri Rajendravarman had a son, lotus of this celestial wave which is the royal race: he was the victorious king Sri Jayavarmadeva." This prince, who became king of Angkor in 968, is described in the inscriptions of Prasat Komphus as "brown, young, with eyes like lotuses and feet marked with lotuses... with beautiful hands marked with the wheel, rich in talents set afire by Sri."

The moral portrait is no less flattering, "Perfectly correct, possessing wealth... gifted with an excellent wisdom, he shone like another Vishnu... strong, courageous, pleasant in his speech." The stele of Vat Sithor emphasizes his goodness, "like an adoring father with his children, he dried the tears of his afflicted subjects with outstretched hands".
The moral portrait emphasizes the virtues of the

sovereign which would guarantee peace and good order in the kingdom. The physical description brings to light certain particularities, such as the hands adorned with the wheel, symbols which the Shakravartin kings must have on their bodies.

Jayavarman V was very young when he acceded to the throne. Several upper dignitaries, who had played an important part in his father's reign, were given even greater attributions. Among them, we find the king's brother in law, the brahmin Divakarabhatta, although the one who held the most power was certainly the brahmin Yajniavaraha. This individual was a member of the Cambodian upper aristocracy since his mother was a daughter of Harshavarman I who had married a brahmin.

7. Yajñiavaraha, founder of Banteay Srei

The person whose name is associated with the founding of the temple of Banteay Srei was a learned brahmin. The inscription of Sek Ta Tuy says of him, "this brahmin-kshatriya, named Yajnavaraha, who had seen the other shore of the sciences, he who holds the title of professor of Shaivism and of first guru to the king of Cambodia". It is he who governed during Jayavarman V's youth, "whose every act he countersigned". When the king came of age, Yajnavaraha's influence remained, apparently, unchanged as the king, "solicited by his guru and having his heart always tending in his favour", rendered the edicts which were more or less suggested to him. It is therefore not surprising that an individual who played such a key role in the kingdom would have built a temple such as Banteay Srei. The temple of Banteay Srei is, justifiably, one of the most celebrated of the Angkor group. It is situated at approximately thirty kilometres to the north-east of the city, near the Stung Siem Reap, in a centre which was then called Isvapura, the "City of the Lord (Shiva)". Founded in 967, shortly before the death of Rajendravarman, it was completed under his son's reign. It is dedicated to the god Shiva, venerated under the name Tribhuvanamahesvara, the "Great Lord of the Three Worlds". The temple is of pink sandstone which presents the peculiarity of being of diminishing proportions as one approaches the central sanctuary. After having penetrated the temple by the eastern entrance, whose dimensions are that of all monuments of that time, as one travels through the successive precincts, one walks through smaller and smaller passages, so small that one may not enter the central sanctuary without bending down. This miniaturization, coupled with the opulence of the decor, led to an equating of Banteay Srei with a jewel.

The temple is edified according to a axial plan whose elements are laid out, more or less symmetrically, on either side of a median axis extending from the eastern exterior gopura to the western exterior gopura, crossing through the central sanctuary. This layout is significantly different from the centralized plan of the temple-mountains such as Phnom Bakheng or Pre Rup.

The central sanctuary, flanked by two lateral sanctuaries, is preceded by a cult room, in accordance with a plan inherited from India. The whole is elevated on a common terrace measuring 0.9 metres high. To the east of the terrace, symmetrical with respect to the axis, rise two kiosks, the "libraries" which were no doubt types of small chapels where perhaps texts or cultural materials were stored. All of these edifices are reunited in an initial enclosure[7]. Banteay Srei is surrounded by four enclosures pierced with passages to the east and to the west. As in the majority of Khmer temples, these passages are entry pavilions, or gopura, which sheltered holy images.

Banteay Srei's decor is especially refined. The pink sandstone lends itself beautifully to the carvings. The artists, authors of these works, achieved a veritable tour de force in their accumulation of sculptures, while at the same time avoiding an overload of motifs. Be they masculine, the dvarapala, or feminine, the devata, the guardian figures sculpted in the walls radiate youth and elegance.

On the dados of the libraries and the gopura, scenes were substituted for the vegetal decor, animated by a single divine figure which adorns the tympanum of earlier monuments. For the first time in the 10th century, we have before our eyes, in Banteay Srei, people depicted in various moments in their existence, meditating, fighting, or advancing through the forest. On the two dados of the southern library, Shiva seated on Kailasa, rests on a graded pyramid, analogous to those of the temples, and symbolizing the mountain. In the northern library, there is a scene depicting the god Indra unleashing a tropical storm on the forest, to the great joy of men and animals. On this same kiosk, the western dado shows Krishna killing King Kamsa in his palace. The wealth of the sculpted images on Banteay Srei is to be found not only in their beauty and in the harmony of their composition, but also in their profound human significance whose sensitivity emanates from the figures. Moreover, this is the first depiction we have of Cambodian life in the second half of the 10th century.

8. The city of Angkor at the end of the tenth century

When Rajendravarman re-established residence in Angkor, he erected sanctuaries on the outskirts of the city which had been traced by his uncle Yashovarman. In founding the Phimeanakas, he set the Royal Palace in the northern part of Yashodharapura. The Phimeanakas is placed on the city's north-south axis. The Royal Palace's gopura must have been edified in the third quarter of the 10th century, as may be postulated according to certain decorative details (devatas in the Banteay Srei style). Across from the Royal Palace, probably at the same time as the gopura, were erected the two long buildings of the northern and southern Khleang; behind the northern Khleang there already existed a small temple in the Banteay Srei style.

Three groups of edifices emerge from this era: in the centre of the first Yassodapura, the Phnom Bakheng, the Baksei Chamkrong and Prasat Bei. In the northern part of the city, the Royal Palace and a few monuments surrounding the Great Square; finally, to the east, on the city's outskirts, the Eastern Mebon, Pre Rup, Prasat Kravan and Bat Chum. To these temples must be added the small sanctuaries of Prasat Prah Enkosei. As for the Banteay Srei temple, although it belongs to what we now refer to as the "Angkor group", it was in Isvapura, an agglomeration outside of Yashodharapura.

We know nothing of the houses of the ordinary inhabitants of Angkor, nor how they were laid out in the city. A dado of Banteay Srei can be found in King Kamsa's palace in Mathura. This opulent home consists of a pavilion raised on piles which support the floor of the living space. Krishna killed Kamsa in the great room which was flanked by two smaller rooms with lower ceilings. This is the refuge of the weeping women from the palace. In spite of the elevated superstructures, the palace had only a single storey. Above the lateral rooms, however, there existed small lodges which were apparently habitable as we see faces at the windows of these attic rooms. The architecture was probably of ornately sculpted wood. The ceiling of the main room appears to be covered with a type of velum. Garlands hang from the beams of the lateral rooms and between the piles.

It is entirely possible that certain pavillons, in the king's palace and in the homes of the aristocracy, had a layout similar to that which is found in traditional modern architecture. As for the everyday life of the inhabitants of Angkor during that era, rich or poor, we are left to surmise. The first scenes depicting daily activities would not appear in the bas-reliefs until the end of the 11th century.

1 Banteay Srei, southern sanctuary, outbuilding
of the central sanctuary, gopura I east,
southern library, (2nd half 10th cent.)

2 Banteay Srei, northern sanctuary, western face,
southern devata (female guardian),
(2nd quarter 10th cent.)

3 Banteay Srei, northern library, western pediment,
"Kamsa is killed by Krishna",
(2nd quarter 10th cent.),

4 Banteay Srei, statue of Umamahesvara
(Shiva and Uma), Banteay Srei style
(Phnom Penh National Museum),
(3rd quarter 10th cent.)

CHAPTER III

ANGKOR UNDER THE DYNASTY
OF SURYAVARMAN I (1002-1080)

1. The reign of Udayadityavarman I (1001-1002)

Jayavarman V died in 1001. He was barely over forty, and left no descendants. The crown was handed on to one of his relatives, Prince Udayadityavarman I, "The one whose armour is the rising sun". The new king was the nephew of one of the deceased sovereign's wives. The inscriptions in Skok Kak Thom does not even mention Udayadityavarman I, whose reign lasted only a year, as he died in 1002. There exist, neither in Angkor nor elsewhere, no works which may be attributed to him.

Udayadityavarman's right to the throne was no doubt contested and, during his very brief reign, dissension erupted. His death marked the beginning of a battle for succession which was to last for close to ten years, and which ended in the founding of a new dynasty.

2. Jayavîravarman and the battle for succession

Of the two pretenders to the throne who had likely ceded during Udayadityavarman's reign, one, Jayavîravarman, appears to have reigned immediately in Angkor; the other, Suryavarman, was forced to wait a number of years before conquering the capital, although the future would belong to him and his sons.

Considered a usurper, unsung on the stele of Sdok Kak Thom, perhaps ousted from Angkor in 1006, Jayaviravarman did leave his mark on Khmer epigraphy, however. Nothing tells us whether he had a right to the throne, nor whether he attempted to legitimize his hold on power. The inscription in the Prasat Trapeang Run states simply,

"Having his golden stool tarnished by the pollen of the garlands of flowers (which crown) the heads of all bowing kings, King Sri Jayaviravarman took possession of the earth in 924."

This date, expressed in Indian saka, corresponds to the year 1002. The same inscription, after having praised his beauty, lauds his knowledge saying that "the example of the many channeled Ganga Science flowed straight into this ocean of many qualities". He ruled in the Angkor region between 1003 and 1006, but we do not know upon what date he was ousted by his most fortunate rival.

In order to solidify his power, Jayaviravarman sought to obtain the support of the upper dignitaries by giving them gifts of land or by reconfirming previous endowments. Concerned with keeping goods and powers obtained during previous reigns, several high dignitaries rallied around him. His gifts were no doubt contested as, more than once, the inscriptions mention that markers which had been unearthed had to be replanted.

3. Jayaviravarman's foundations

Founding a temple and assuring one's edification constituted a royal act.

It was supposed that the Phimeanakas could have been built by Jayaviravarman, but this temple's pyramid seems to come from an earlier time. J. Boisselier is willing to accept the temple of Ta Keo, a monument to the east of Angkor, as being Jayaviravarman's work. Ta Keo is associated with the Hemasringagiri, the "Mount of the Golden Horn", a term which is sometimes used to designate Mount Meru. An inscription discovered in Ta Keo, issued by a high dignitary by the name of Yogisvarapandita, who was in the service of Suryavarman I, says that this former worked for the king who, "completed Hemasringagiri". If Ta Keo does indeed correspond to Hemasringagiri, it would have been completed by Suryavarman I but, in reality, Ta Keo, which is an important temple, was never completed, its decor being only barely begun.

G. Coedès thought to have found an explanation for the unfinished state of Ta Keo, in this same inscription. The text recounts how lightning struck Hemasringagiri, and how Yogisvarapandita performed a ceremony which was to be expiatory; it indicates that this dignitary began the completion of the prasat, "by purchasing stones". Lightning striking the monument would explain why the work was left incomplete. The inscription states, however, that work on the temple continued after the accident. J. Boisselier concludes that it is a mistake to identify the Hemasringagiri with Ta Keo, and that the non completion of the latter had another cause. He believes that Jayaviravarman's eviction explains the abandonment of this temple whose construction the king had undertaken. In his opinion, as in that of L.P. Briggs, the Hemasringagiri is not Ta Keo but rather the Phimeanakas[8] .

In its architecture, its style and the materials used for its construction, Ta Keo is truly a royal foundation. Its high pyramid sporting five grades supporting five staggered towers is made entirely of sandstone. There is not a royal stele to be found, however. The inscriptions speak only of the activities of the dignitaries, under the orders of Suryavarman I. This king could neither abandon nor take as his own the vanquished rival's principal foundation.

It was therefore logical that the guard and upkeep of the temple be conferred on a handful of upper dignitaries.

Because of its non completion, Ta Keo is an austere temple, admirable for the purity of its proportions. The first of all Khmer temples, it contains outbuildings for each of the four entries to principal sanctuaries and, on the second grade of the pyramid, a surrounding gallery which is interrupted only at the corners by passageways. It was once believed that Khmer architecture owed its esthetic value to its decor. The Ta Keo temple, which is almost devoid of all sculpture, proves that this architecture is endowed with proportions and a purity of line which attains a summit of perfection.

4. Suryavarman I (1002-1050)

At a date which will never be specified, but which may be supposed to be somewhere between 1006 and 1010, Jayaviravarman disappeared definitively from the Cambodian political scene. Suryavarman I remained as sole sovereign.

Who was this man, Jayaviravarman's most fortunate rival? The inscription of Kuk Pring Chrum praises him thus:

"There was this king, Sri Suryavarman, armour come from the solar race, adornment of the royal condition, gifted with the brilliance of many suns...

He was a Kubera in his liberality, an ocean of stability, a sun of splendour, a lion of heroism, a moon of beauty, a master of science."[9]

We do not know which rights he evoked in order to present himself for the throne. One inscription says only that, "come from the maternal lineage of Sri Indravarman who issued from a princely lineage, he adorned the succession of kings." Even if this genealogy is authentic, Suryavarman is from a family other than that of his predecessors. He is related to King Harshavarman I through his wife Viralakshmi, who may have been Jayaviravarman's widow. Suryavarman would have married her in order to legitimize his accession to the throne.

It was suggested arbitrarily that he was Malaysian in origin, a supposition which is based on Chi'eng Mai's chronicles which narrate the intervention, in the Menam basin in Lopburi, of a certain Kambujaraja, son of the sovereign of a Malaysian kingdom. It was thought that Suryavarman I had exclusive domain over central Thailand. It is certain that he was interested in this region, and the inscriptions from the time of his reign tell of Khmer domination in the Lopburi region. It does appear that he sought to impose his authority on the ancient kingdom of Dvaravati, which disintegrated after having extended itself over a large part of the Menam basin.

Suryavarman considered that he had become king of Cambodia in 1002, upon Udayadityavarman's death, and that Jayaviravarman's reign was nothing more than an accident which had kept him away from Angkor, during the first part of his reign. It is perhaps due to these ten years of war, which kept him far from his kingdom, that he took such a great interest in the provinces. His greatest foundations are not to be found in Angkor. It appears that the grandest sanctuary of his dynasty is the temple of Prah Vihear on the Dangrek. Elevated on the edge of a plateau which dominates the Cambodian plain, this temple is an admirable monument to which Suryavarman I magically transferred the god Bhadresvara, the divinity of Wat Phu.

5. Works executed in Angkor under the reign of Suryavarman I

No major construction was undertaken in Angkor during Suryavarman's reign, although religious life in the temples was in no way interrupted. The king was obliged to favour the prosperity of his predecessors' foundations. It is for this reason that falling short of completing Ta Keo, he would have entrusted its upkeep to dignitaries. Having no doubt established his principal temple outside of Angkor, Suryavarman I focused his works on the Royal Palace. It is probable that he built the vaulted gallery on the grades of the Phimeanakas which served as an enclosure. If the Hemasringagiri is indeed the Phimeanakas, this construction could have taken place after the monument was struck by lightning.

6. Pacification

Throughout his lengthy reign, Suryavarman had the task of pacifying a nation which had been torn apart by nine years of civil war, and to reconstruct that which had been demolished or abandoned. The pacification appears to have been complete, since,

"under this sovereign's reign, the men who fell asleep alone in the forest no longer feared being robbed."

Reestablishing order in the country was not sufficient, however; he had also to assure himself that the troubles would not re-erupt. The goal of his provincial foundations was to establish the king's power over the Orientals. Yet another necessity was to render unwavering all of his subjects' devotion to the State.

In order to preserve their property, the dignitaries were tempted to rally round a rebel, even if he were only temporarily in power. It is for this reason that Suryavarman engraved, on the piers of the Royal Palace's gopura, the text of the oath of fidelity which several categories of ministers had to swear before the king. In the Cambodian monarchy, the tradition of pronouncing an annual oath to the sovereign was maintained, in addition to which the modern day text has remained, in its substance, very similar to the one sworn in the 11th century. It is without a doubt that the Royal Palace of Angkor already practiced the solemn ceremony which has survived to present. The text of the oath given to Suryavarman I was written in clearly Brahminic terms, whereas the current text is of a Buddhist leaning.

7. End of Suryavarman I's reign

It was thought that Suryavarman was Buddhist, according to interpretations of his posthumous name, Nirvanapada. All of his foundations were Brahminic, however. While it is true that a Buddhist monarch may create Brahminic foundations, J. Filliozat points out that the posthumous name of Nirvanapada could also be applied to a Shaivist.

Suryavarman I died in 1050, after a reign which lasted close to fifty years. This lengthy rule allowed him to establish a dynasty. Upon his death, he left behind two sons who would succeed him: Udayadityavarman II and Harshavarman III.

8. The Khmer monarchy under Suryavarman I's sons (1050-1080)

Udayadityavarman II was the son of Suryavarman I and Queen Viralakshmi who was perhaps first married to Jayaviravarman. The new king had received the proper education for an heir to the throne:

"His Majesty studied all areas of knowledge, beginning with the sciences, grammar, law, and all the other sastras." The text on the stele of Sdok Kak Thom adds, "his spirit was stimulated by his many talents, mechanical arts and others".

One of his father's dignitaries, Jayendrapandita, was his spiritual master. It was he who prepared the sacrament for his religious initiation. Although the inscription of Sdok Kak Thom states that, "his kingdom delighted in his talents" and, "he made hearts bloom", his reign was troubled by numerous revolts which were crushed by General Sangrama. It is difficult to establish the causes of the unrest, which appears to have been quite marked as it extended to the outer reaches of Angkor.

These revolts were the cause of widespread destruction and, from the moment of his ascension in 1066,

Harshavarman had the task of extracting his country from the ruins of this trouble period. He was obliged not only to restore his country but also to assume military operations against the Chams, his neighbours to the east. The brahmin Divakarapandita began his dignitary career under this reign. His ambitious manoeuverings were to weigh on Cambodian politics for the next thirty years.

9. Foundations of Suryavarman's sons in Angkor

In spite of the difficulties which Udayadityavarman encountered during his sixteen-year reign, he managed to construct major foundations in Angkor. His name will be forever associated with the Baphuon temple, as well as with the artificial lake known as the Western baray.

An inscription celebrates the foundation of Baphuon: "Seeing the Golden Mountain (the Meru) rise at the centre of the Jambudvipa, or house of the gods, it was done... a mountain of gold at the heart of his city. At the summit of this golden mountain, in a golden temple of celestial brilliance, he erected a "golden" Shiva-linga".

The Baphuon was not at the geometric centre of Yashodhapura, although it appears that the northern limits of Yashovarman's city have always been imprecise. For the previous one hundred years, the political centre of the city had been the group of buildings belonging to the Royal Palace. The Baphuon, like the Royal Palace, opened up onto Angkor's Great Square whose vast esplanade stretched eastward to the two edifices of Khleang. The Baphuon rises next to the Royal Palace.

Baphuon's central sanctuary has been destroyed, and no vestiges remain. It is a unique sanctuary, built at the summit of a pyramid whose grades support three galleries forming enclosures which open up at the corners into corridor pavilions. The walls of these gopura are covered with bas-reliefs, set out in small, superimposed scenes depicting myths and various epic tales. We find young Krishna's feats, as well as a number of episodes from the Ramayana. These scenes are of a marvellous elegance. Extremely varied, the reliefs of Baphuon illustrate animals and men, battles and scenes of palace life. This is the first time in which images sculpted on a temple wall allow us to catch a glimpse of life in Cambodia.

As the Baphuon is Udayadityavarman II's principal temple, it was here that General Sangrama came to pay homage by offering the spoils of war taken from vanquished rebels.

10. The Western baray

To the east of Angkor, Udayadityavarman mounted a dyke which encircled a reservoir measuring 8 km by 2.2 km. It was thought that the eastern baray was drying up and that a new construction was necessary. It is possible that, at that time, the eastern baray was indeed diminishing, but this would not have been the sole reason for creating another artificial lake. Udayadityavarman no doubt also wished to create a tirtha, or sacred lake, to the west, as Yashovarman had done to the east. In the centre of the Western baray, the king edified a temple, the Western Mebon, whose adornment consists of small bas-reliefs which recall Baphuon. Next to Mebon, the bust of a colossal bronze statue of Vishnu in repose was found. The technique employed for this piece, which is now housed in the Phnom Penh National Museum, is magnificent. In spite of its deteriorated state, it continues to bear witness to the perfection achieved by the Khmers in the sculpting of bronze during the 11th century.

11. End of Suryavarman I's dynasty

King Harshavarman III died in 1080. His successor, Jayavarman VI, was in no way related to him. He belonged to the Mahidharapura family, an apparently wealthy clan from northern Cambodia.

12. Angkor and the end of the eleventh century

In the city at this time, only the temples from the 10th and 11th century, as well as Baphuon and the buildings linked with the Royal Palace, were made of stone. The king's home, like those of his subjects, had to be of perishable materials. The small bas-reliefs of Baphuon illustrate some images of typical houses of the era. As in the tympan of Banteay Srei, however, these pictures represent scenes from mythological and epic tales which take place in the homes of the wealthy. One would have to wait until the mid-12th century before finding artists' renderings of peasant life. The architectural styles, which are also represented on the walls of Baphuon, are not doubt reproductions of certain pavilions which were to be found within the walls of the Royal Palace.

In the northern gopura II of Baphuon, there is an integral representation of the celestial palace. It consists of a long, horizontal structure, prolonged by vestibules. The roof of the vestibules is lower than that of the central part. As in the Cams palace represented at Banteay Srei, the entire roof rests on columns: there are no walls but rather drapes hanging down between the pillars. On the side of the building, pediments top the architrave's of the principal traves. The roof is covered with circular tiles, and its peak is adorned with a row of spikes. This style would be reproduced throughout Cambodian architecture. Did houses enclosed by walls or wooden panels exist? It seems likely enough even though none are depicted, as all scenes took place in the Royal Palace.

As far as can be ascertained, the furniture was quite simple, consisting mainly of low seats resting on four legs on which it was only possible to sit either cross-legged or with one foot dangling. These seats were reserved for people of upper rank, or for venerated ascetics.

The Royal Palace and some of the homes belonging to princes were lavishly decorated. The stele of Sdok Kak Thom describes brahmin Jayendrapandita's palace thus:

"This palace was embellished with statues of sculpted stone, very appealing, and covered with a scenery adorned with female figures; how could one imagine beauty otherwise?"

All of the bas-reliefs leave us to surmise regarding scenes of street life. Next to a group of men, a horse-drawn cart with a driver and two passengers approaches. In another scene, an elephant advances slowly and, further on, two commoners are bartering next to an oxen cart filled with produce, most probably fruit. The two cart drivers are clad in ordinary loincloths, whereas the gods' haunches are enveloped with elegant and finely pleated fabric. This garment was draped in the same manner as a modern day sampot with the panels knotted in front, passed through the thighs and pinned in the back. Although the sculptors of Baphuon were not ordered to depict scenes of everyday life, they did, however, suggest an aspect of contemporary society upon which the inscriptions shed some light.

13. Society

It appears that a veritable gorge separated the nobility from the populace. There is frequent mention in the inscriptions of the Brahminic caste. The term Kshatriya is only rarely cited, however, and appears to have been reserved to members of the royal family. Between those belonging to these two upper castes, matrimonial unions were frequent. We have examples of the close ties which existed between the aristocratic castes: Yajniavaraha, born of the marriage between the daughter of King Harshavarman I and a brahmin or, again, Divarakarabhatta, an Indian brahmin, husband of one of Jayavarman V's sisters.

We have seen the role which was played by certain prominent individuals. The Brahmins performed religious tasks centred around the king which allowed them a marked influence on Angkoran Cambodia's both religious and political life.

It is difficult to ascertain whether all those who received distinctions belonged to the upper castes. Although they came from wealthy social classes, many of the state's servants were neither Brahmins nor Kshatriya. There are examples of ministers who achieved high rank through merit. The king's favour extended not only to administrators and warriors. An inscription in Vat Baset, regarding goods and honours bestowed on an artist by King Udayatiyavarman II states:

"By order of the king, he was (promoted to the order of)

Visvakarman, chief of the artists... Upon the occasion of the completion of his works, the king conferred upon him a property from
his own estate which would be exempt from contest for all time...
Having assembled the Brahmins and princes as witnesses, the king
charged the President of the Court to plant the five markers of this
property... Out of consideration for the Visvakarman's virtues, the
king ordered the inscription of this property with the family in the
celebrated caste of the people, keepers of the golden cup."

Hence, an example of the ennoblement of a family.

The commoners formed an inferior mass of whose
social importance we know very little. They were subject to various obligations such as taxes and labour.
The least known caste was that of the artisans and, in a
general sense, the commoners. In the inscribed texts,
be they on the stelae or the bas-reliefs, we find enume-
rated long lists of slaves offered to the foundations. The
most humble among them were the "slaves to build the
rice fields". At a slightly higher grade we find the spe-
cialized slaves: all manual labourers, cooks in particular, the spinners and weavers. Finally, among the privileged, we find the parasol bearers, musicians, dancers
and singers. The construction of the temples must have
employed servile labour to cut the stones, to transport
and lay them in place, as well as for the preparation and
baking of the bricks, and the extraction and drying of
the laterite. This labour would also have been used for
irrigation works, for dyke construction and for digging
canals and reservoirs.

G. Coedès revealed the existence of names attributed to slaves in the inscriptions such as "Dog" or

"Stench", and even "Loathsome". It is thus obvious that slaves were an object of general scorn. There are, however, less contemptuous designations such as "Despising injustice" or "Who does not reveal all"; there is even mention of a woman known as "Born to love". It must be noted, however, that Cambodians are wont to give humorous surnames which may appear irreverent, and this, even among the aristocracy.

14. The king

The multitudinous praises which the inscriptions bestowed upon the king were not mere flattery; it was considered a royal duty to possess all celebrated qualities. According to the Indian ideal of monarchy, he was the kingdom's head servant, the preserver of law and order, the shepherd of his people... His power was confined by adherence to the laws of the land.

The sovereign obtained royalty through inheritance from either his father or from another relative. The inscriptions speak often of rights to the throne obtained through ancestral heritage, especially in the case of contested successions.

The names attributed to the king, to the princes and upper dignitaries is preceded by the word "Sri", or Fortunate One. In Old Khmer we find the sovereign's name preceded by the tittle "Vrah Pada", or Sacred Feet, which is generally translated as, His Majesty.

After his death, the king takes on a posthumous designation. Those whom their successors considered as being usurpers did not receive this honour. The king's foundations, however, regardless of the sovereign's legitimacy, were respected by the successors and, as we have seen, the king may charge upper dignitaries with their maintenance.

The various donations and confirmations of property, according to the inscriptions, proved that the king had the prerogative of offering land. As concerns legislation, he was supreme justice, although his edicts were obliged to adhere to the established order.

The inscription of Pre Rup defines the king's duties thus:
stanza CCXCV:

"O, ye who achieve royalty, be forever one with the Dharma[11] , excellent in your virtuous liberality, eminent by your majesty, rich in treasures and armies, as were the ancient kings."

The same inscriptions bids the kings maintain the foundations built by their predecessors,
stanza CCXCI:

"O, ye who are plunged luxuriously in this sleep which is the joy of royal privilege, if this work were to collapse, awaken in its favour like Narayana[12] (sleeping) in the Ocean of Milk."

15. Administration

The king was surrounded by a few high dignitaries which he chose from the upper castes. Certain ministers took care of all of the palace's services. There was the head of the guards of the royal chamber, the head of personal secretaries, the inspector of the royal bed, the head servant in charge of all royal insignias: the crown, earrings, bracelets, necklaces, etc. The inscriptions mention the head of the royal storerooms many times. Certain ministers were in charge of the dead. Among them there was the individual in charge of funerary rites, although the duties associated with the dead were not limited to the funerary; it principally entailed the maintenance of the foundations undertaken by the defunct or those built in their honour. There were also inspectors, or executors or the defunct's worldly goods, which would be donated to a temple or monastery.

The text of the oath sworn by the Suryavarman I's officers mention titles which do not appear to correspond to any particular title, and which must belong to elite officers. Among them, we find the titles sanjak and tamrvac. G. Coedès postulated that the title of sanjak,

"designated those dignitaries who enjoyed the king's utmost confidence, a devotion which implied a willingness to absolute self-sacrifice." The title of tamrvac was bestowed on lesser people. G. Coedès supposed that they must have comprised a sort of elite guard from which the king chose his men of confidence.

Apart from the titles, the officers obtained honorary symbols from the king which were, with regards to most privileged individuals, palanquins and parasols. Palanquins were reserved for princes and very high dignitaries. The shafts were covered with either gold or silver, according to an individual's importance. The number of parasols, which were borne during solemn proceedings, reflected the minister's dignity. They were multi-tiered and made of embroidered fabric.

16. The Court

The king was surrounded by the royal family and the members of the Court. In the inscriptions, the queen is often spoken of as part of the king's wealth. It is certain that a princess's lineage could transmit rights to the throne, be it to her husband or son. It seems that no other image could better depict the royal couple than the statues of Umamahesvara, in particular those found at Banteay Srei which depict Uma seated on Shiva's knees, sharing in his power and grandeur. After the queen came the secondary wives and concubines.

The Court's splendour was unfurled during royal festivities.

The coronation not only conferred a religious character on the king, but also gave him the opportunity to display his magnificence.

The inscriptions do not describe the ceremony, but they do indicate two essential moments: the Initiation, or diksha, and the Anointment, or abhisheka. Every year, the king's coronation was commemorated by a ceremony whose goal was to guard the kingdom from famine and epidemics. During this ceremony, the abhisheka was renewed. The inscription of Pre Rup recounts that, "each month of Pushya, the king is anointed with ambrosial waters which fall from one hundred ewers polished by time".

A number of regular festivals took place during the year as did certain extraordinary festivities, such as those given upon the king's victorious return from battle, which would similarly filled the capital with jubilance.

1 Prasat Ta Keo, unfinished temple, (early 11th cent.)

2 Baphuon, Udayadityavarman II's royal temple,
(3rd quarter 11th cent.),

3 Baphuon, bas-relief, (3rd quarter 11th cent.)

4 Fragment of a colossal statue of Vishnu in repose,
bronze, (National Museum of Phnom Penh),
discovered in the Western Mebon,
(3rd quarter 11th cent.)

CHAPTER IV

SURYAVARMAN II (1113 - APPROX. 1144) AND THE FOUNDATION OF ANGKOR VAT

1. Advent of Suryavarman II

We know very little of what took place in Angkor between the disappearance of Harshavarman III in 1080 and the advent of Suryavarman II in 1113. It was thought that Jayavarman VI may have reigned in northern Cambodia, whereas Harshavarman III's successor ruled in Angkor. The text on the Prah Khan stele states, however,

stanza XIII: "Having obtained supreme rule in the holy city of Yashodharapura, after having vanquished the throng of enemies, King Jayavarmadeva, whose family lived in Mahidharapura, planted in all directions, right up to the sea of the pillars of glory.[13] "

It is certain that the country was divided at the beginning of the 12th century. We know that Suryavarman II seized the power from two kings one of whom was his uncle, Dharanindravarman I, who had succeeded his brother Jayavarman VI, "without having desired royalty". During a dramatic duel against his nephew, the prince was, "stripped of his royalty".

2. Suryavarman II

At his advent, Suryavarman II emerges as an ambitious prince who, "still young, coming to the end of his studies, manifested a desire for the royal dignity of his family". Untiring conqueror, he bore arms against his neighbouring enemies throughout his forty year reign, not only in the Menam basin, but also against the Chams to the east, and even against the Dai-Viet, in what is now known as Vietnam. Relations with China were re-established under his reign, and several ambassadors were sent to the emperor who conferred "high honours" on Suryavarman.

The so called "historical" bas-relief at Angkor Vat contains three depictions of Suryavarman II, using his posthumous name "Paramavishnuloka". These representations are not merely portraits, although they correspond admirably with the image one might have of Suryavarman II. In the western part of the bas-relief, dominating all those who come to pay homage, the seated king extends his left arm in an authoritative gesture. A little further on he is again represented, this time leaving for war, then standing on his elephant in the middle of his generals, surrounded by parasols, fly-chasers, banners, and accompanied by cavaliers.

For the third time, Divakaparandita, become Suryavarman's spiritual master, oversaw the coronation. Upon this occasion he was showered with gifts from the new king and was put in charge of a pilgrimage to all of the principal temples of the land, bearing offerings from the monarch. The inscriptions tell of the foundations made in the many great sanctuaries, Wat Phu, Prah Vihear and Banteay Srei. This spiritual master must have been quite elderly by then, and probably passed away during that reign. The king's favour which he enjoyed was such that the inscription of Prah Vihear presents him in these terms: "Sri Divakarapandita, whose foot rested on the diadem which crowned the head of Sri Suryavarman, master of the world".

3. The temple of Angkor Vat

The only temple in Angkor which may be attributed to Suryavarman II with absolute certainty is Angkor Vat, the most prestigious monument in Khmer art. It is with Angkor Vat that the concept of the mountain-temple achieved its apex.

Surrounded by its moat, the Angkor Vat group covers close to 200 hectares. The temple is at the south-east corner of the first Yashodharapura, whose earthen rampart no doubt still existed at the beginning of the 16th century. Angkor Vat faces west. Access is gained through the Western Entranceways, at the far end of the path which crosses the moats. In the other temples no gopura achieve the scope of the Western Entranceways to Angkor Vat. At either side of the triple, central passage stretch long galleries terminating in two large carriage-gates known as "the Elephant Gates". Behind the Western Entranceways extends the 350-metre long Grand Path, which leads to the Cruciform Terrace, then to the temple itself, rising up on a high pyramid, and surrounded by three galleries.

Around the Central Sanctuary, four corner sanctuaries are linked by a gallery, forming the first enclosure; in the corners, four covered courtyards link this gallery to the Central Sanctuary. To the west, between the second and third sanctuary, lies the Cruciform Courtyard.

Under the third enclosure's gallery, whose perimeter measures over 800 metres, the wall is covered with bas-reliefs, the most celebrated of Khmer sculpture. This long fresco of reliefs is interrupted only by the corner pavilions and gopura. Only the north-east quadrant of these bas-reliefs was not finished during Suryavarman II's time, although the first lines of the remaining works may have been chiseled. We will see, further on, under what circumstances the sculpting was completed during the 16th century.

4. Angkor Vat's iconography

Angkor Vat's iconography is entirely dedicated to the glory of Vishnu, Suryavarman II's divinity of predilection, and whose name he assumed posthumously: Paramavishnuloka. On the pediments, the lintels and even at the base of the pillars, there are multitudinous depictions of the god and his avatars, or descents on earth, in human or animal form. It is above all the reliefs of the third enclosure which illustrate the great Vishnuist legends.

On the walls of the western gallery, on either side of the passages leading to the Cruciform Courtyard, the sculptors recounted the final battles of the two famous Indian epics: the Ramayana and the Mahabharata. To the north, the victory at Lanka marks the triumph of Rama, Vishnu's incarnation. To the south, the battle of Kurukshetra, the final episode of the Mahabharata, won by the Pandava, Krishna's allies, another of Vishnu's avatars. In the southeastern gallery, a marvellously majestic composition contains the myth of the churning of the Sea of Milk by the gods, combining their forces to oppose the enemy asura. The goal of the churning was to extract the nectar of everlasting life from the water.

In the western section, the wall of the southern gallery is covered with the previously mentioned "historical bas-reliefs". In this section are depicted the judgement of the dead and their passage to Paradise or Hell. As is the case for all of the bas-reliefs, the execution of this composition is admirable. Although stretching long over the surfaces, the scenes are all highly gripping.

Bas-reliefs cover the walls of the two corner pavilions of the western face. They lack the grandeur of the compositions which adorn the galleries, and are mainly focused on episodes from the myths of Rama and Krishna, as well as a number featuring Shiva. The arrangement of the scenes is extremely elegant although these less solemn images left an opening for the artists' to express their personal sensibilities, and even fantasies.

On either side of these entrances, on the walls of the gopura, the sanctuaries and even the windows of the upper galleries, we find a multitude of sculpted devata. These female deities, protectors of the temple, appear in other monuments as gracious guardians, isolated in niches. In Angkor Vat, they are in groups in two, three or more. Sometimes smiling, sometimes serious, they appear to be communing with each other. Their costumes and adornment is extremely varied, reflecting, perhaps, the dress of the day in various Cambodian regions, as well as the fashion of the young women of Angkor. As were Krishna's sixteen thousand wives, the devata are in the service of the god, lord of the temple.

5. Angkor Vat and the significance of the mountain-temple

Angkor Vat constitutes the epitome of the mountain-temple; a veritable Meru whose five summits rise to a height of over sixty metres.

Under the Central Sanctuary, archeological digs revealed the existence of a well which descends to ground level. At the bottom of the well, a foundation consisting of gold disks[14] was found.

It was thought that the existence of a central well may have been linked to the cult of the dead. Angkor Vat does indeed present a layout which may be associated with a funerary monument. Its main entrance opens onto the west, the cardinal point of the dead[15]. Moreover, in order to follow the sequence of the bas-reliefs in the third enclosure, one must run the full circle of the monument, keeping to the left; a circumambulation reserved to the funerary rite known as prasvya. All of these peculiarities led G. Coedès to postulate: were these Khmer monuments, raised on high bases, temples or tombs[16] ?

In several Khmer monuments, long, narrow stone vats

were found, sometimes lidded and pierced with a drain at the base. The shape of these vats recalls that of a sarcophagus. At Banteay Samre, a highly stylized vat was found whose lid contained a rather large, square hole adorned with mouldings; at the base of the vat the orifice is embellished with the head of a monster. This vat is not long enough to contain a supine cadaver. G. Coedès surmised that it may have contained a cadaver placed in a foetal position. It is thus that, in present day Cambodia, the body of a prince or a king is placed in a funerary urn before cremation. The hole pierced at the base may have been a sanitation drain for bodily fluids; the orifice in the lid may have been used for the insertion of a strip of gauze which, during funerary rites, is used to unite the dead with the members of the funeral party. Thus, even if these vats were only temporary repositories for cadavers awaiting cremation, they did play a role within the funerary monument. G. Coedès thought that the mountain-temples were at once tombs and sanctuaries in which the posthumously deified deceased were venerated after death.

J. Filliozat saw a link between the shape of the Khmer mountain-temple and that of certain smaller monuments which were elevated on the tombs of the devout who had received the diksha, or initiation, wherein they were associated with Shiva and, after their death, were not to be cremated but rather buried. Agama's Sanskrit texts state how these faithful must be buried, and specify that, on their tomb, it is possible to erect a graded pyramid on which a linga may be placed[17]. A sanctuary may also be built as a container, whose design corresponds to the mountain-temples of Cambodia.

As for the stone vats, nothing proves that their use was funerary. One of them, which is without a lid and adorned with an ornate border, was simply used as a cistern. J. Filliozat noted that, in Indian temples, vats are used to hold devout offerings, particularly oil. The vat at Banteay Samre may also have served this purpose.

The inscriptions state that a king often received the diksha at the time of his coronation, after which he was identified with Shiva and, after his death, his body was not to be cremated. It was possible to mount a pyramid crowned by a sanctuary containing a linga on his tomb. It is impossible to know whether it was obligatory to built a monumental temple on all of the kings' tombs. The edification of a sanctuary above a tomb may help to explain a phrase from the Chinese traveller Chiu Ta-Kuan who came to Cambodia at the end of the 13th century, "the sovereign is buried in a tower"[18].

At Angkor Vat, the problem is more complex. Suryavarman II's tutelary divinity was Vishnu, as his posthumous name of Paramavishuloka confirms. It is no doubt Vishnu who was venerated in the Central Sanctuary, but under what aspect was he represented? For centuries, the Central Sanctuary has no longer housed this god of whom no trace may be found; it is to Buddha that the cult of the upper floor of the temple is devoted. The memory of a funerary monument must have survived in the traditions of the 13th century, since Chiu Ta-Kuan says that he heard tell that, "the tomb of Lu

Pan is at a distance of approximately one li from the southern door, and measures approximately ten li around". P. Pelliot, who published the translation of this text, believes that Lu Pan, a wonderful Chinese artisan, must have been associated by the author with Visvakarman, the Divine Architect, to whom Cambodian legend attributes the construction of Angkor Vat.

6. The monumental style of Angkor Vat

In the Angkor Group, several monuments date back to the 12th century although, in the absence of inscriptions, they may not be attributed to Suryavarman II with absolute certainty. To the east of Angkor, on either side of a path traced in the axis of the Royal Palace, rise the sandstone temples of Thommanon and Chau Say Tevoda. Both contain a sanctuary preceded by a cult room, a library and an enclosure pierced by gopura.

Further on, past the dyke of the western baray, the temple of Banteay Samre strikes an even more imposing figure. Its central sanctuary, preceded by a cult room, is flanked by two libraries and surrounded by a double enclosure. One gains access to the temple by a road bordered with markers leading up to a majestic terrace.

In Angkor Thom, the Prah Pithu T and U are no doubt from this same era. They were erected to the north of the Khleang. As is the case for the three temples built at the outskirts of the city, these are Brahminic sanctuaries. To the north of the Royal Palace stands a monument which also appears to come from the same time period. It is the

Buddhist temple of Prah Palilay whose name recalls a
scene from Buddha's life: the donation made to the
Joyous One by the elephant Parileyya, and by his friend,
the monkey. G. Coedès suggested that the temple of
Prah Palilay may have been built by Jayavarman VI. It
seems difficult however to date it that far back.

The paucity of epigraphic information in these monuments deprives us of indications on the cults and the
divinities who were therein revered. On the whole, it
does not seem possible to date these temples further
back in time than Angkor Vat.

7. Khmer society in the twelfth century, as seen through the bas-reliefs of Angkor Vat

The iconography of the 10th and 11th centuries revealed little of every day Khmer existence. At Angkor Vat,
whereas the "historical bas-relief" depicts the splendour
of a royal procession, the mythological or epic compositions are rife with details inspired by the spectacle of life.

It the western section, the "historical" bas-relief shows
Suryavarman II at the centre of his Court. The king is seated cross-legged, on a seat adorned with a naga. Behind
him stand parasol and fan bearers, as well as fly chasers.
In front of him, a kneeling crowd pays him homage. To
either side are the members of the Court and, among
them, one recognizes the Brahmins. Their long, thin
faces and slender noses reveal their Indian origins. All
have long hair. Some wear luxuriously draped sampots
of richly decorated fabric. These well-dressed Brahmins

are no doubt the upper dignitaries. Other individuals, wearing simple loincloths devoid of all adornment, are the ascetics; one of them is telling his beads.

Above the king, a crowd advances, bearing tribute. The women of the Court are crowned with diadems of precious metal and their shoulders are adorned with opulent necklaces; the offering bearers wear a chain or a simple metal circle around their neck. Even though they are not crowned with jewels, they do have very elaborate hairdos.

After having received the homage and tribute of his subjects, the sovereign prepares his departure from the kingdom. After witnessing the spectacle of the Royal Palace of Angkor, we can follow the procession which must have taken place when Suryavarman, upon leaving Yashodharapura, went to battle against the Chams, the Vietnamese or the Mons of Menam. Perched on their elephants, the warrior chiefs advance solemnly; surrounding them, the horsemen prance and the infantrymen march. At the head of the procession walk strange Mongolian-like warriors. Their exposed hair is adorned with feathers or leaves; they wear skirts embellished with pendants. A brief inscription tells us that what we see is the Siamese contingent. The other warriors often wore odd helmets topped with panaches, bird or animal heads. Bearing a lance and a shield, they usually wear a small dagger on their neck, which hangs from a necklace.

The officers' arms are bows and arrows, shields and the deadly machete with its curved blade and long wooden handle. The chiefs are standing on their elephant's back; the number of parasols surrounding them indicates their rank.

The departure for war had religious connotations, hence we see Brahmins accompanying a sort of arch which the inscriptions tell us is a receptacle for the sacred fire. Finally, since gaiety always finds its way into Cambodian ceremonies, jugglers and buffoons jump and cavort, no doubt to the great amusement of the crowd of spectators.

This extraordinary document which allows us to penetrate into the heart of the capital, is not Angkor Vat's sole testimony to Khmer life in the 12th century. Other bas-reliefs contain scenes from country towns. In one mythical recreation, we see shepherds with their flocks, ascetics conversing in a grotto, and a hunter in the forest. Representations of buildings are rare and consist mainly of elegant pleasure pavilions; peasant dwellings are not depicted at Angkor Vat.

The most beautiful image is without a doubt that of a floating pavilion. It is a magnificent castle junk, with a peaked Chinese-style roof, pierced walls and baluster windows. While the rowers row, men at the back of the boat bet on a cock fight, under the curious eye of a father carrying his two children on his back. In the castle on the junk, two people are playing chess. Up front, buffoons gesticulate near a man who is drinking liqueur from a jar through a straw. In sculpting this junk, the artist no doubt drew his inspiration from a common scene on the Siem Reap river or the Great Lake.

Finally the reliefs offer us several images of family life; here a woman bends down toward a young child; there a man with his son leaning against him. In the absence of a concrete backdrop of the day, the artists have, however, rendered the atmosphere of family life in Cambodia.

8. Religious dominance in Angkor Vat

The apparition of scenes from family and village life may have a link with the development of the Krishna cult. In Angkor Vat, many bas-reliefs show episodes from the youth of this hero who was the incarnation of Vishnu. In the south-east corner pavilion and on several lintels and pillar bases, we see sculpted images of Krishna raising mount Govardhana in order to protect villagers against the storm unleashed by Indra. The development of Krishnaite scenes in no way overshadowed other avatars. Representations of the Ramayana, in particular, hold a considerable place in Angkor Vat's iconography.

Never before had a temple of such importance been dedicated to Vishnu in Cambodia. This new religious orientation must be linked with a philosophical movement which emerged, in India, in the 12th century, and which was illustrated by the theologian Ramanuja.

It appears that, very early on, Angkor Vat's celebrity extended far outside Cambodian borders, and even outside of South-East Asia. From the Kurmapurana, J. Filliozat extracted a text which dealt with the Harivarsha, or "Continent of Hari (Vishnu)". This text may have been an addendum to the original Purana which dates further back than the 12th century. As demonstrated by J. Filliozat, this passage from the Kurmapurana which describes the Vasudeva (Vishnu) sanctuary may well be applied to Angkor Vat[19] :

XLVII
10. "There, shining like the clear moon, like pure crystal, is the sanctuary of Vasudeva, protected by a forest of parijata.
11. "With four incomparable doors, graced with four porticos, and ten enclosures, difficult to climb, difficult to enter.
12. "Endowed with crystal hallways, like the house of the king of the gods, adorned with a thousand gold pillars.
13. "Endowed with golden staircases, embellished with all manner of jewels, endowed with divine thrones, gifted by all beauties.
14-15. "Embellished with ponds and rivers of delicious water, and all filled with yogin entirely devoted to Narayana, pure, all given to the recitation of Veda, meditating... on Hari.
17. "Gracious and ravishing women sing and dance, resplendent with youth, forever devoted to beauty."

It is certain that some descriptions are somewhat exagerated and that the poetry has aggrandized the materials, notably when speaking of crystal and when describing as made of gold elements which were only covered with gold. The gold and jewels have disappeared, but the ascetics seem to meditate still, sculpted at the base of the pillars, and the "gracious and ravishing" devata still animate the temple walls.

1 Angkor Vat, aerial view, (1st half 12th cent.)

2 Angkor Vat, Grand entrance path, gallery
of the bas-reliefs (third enclosure)
and Central Mountain, (1st half 12th cent.)

3 Angkor Vat, Eastern entrances, devata,
(1st half 12th cent.)

4 Angkor Vat, third southern gallery,
so-called "historic" bas-relief, King Suryavarman II,
(1st half 12th cent.)

5 Angkor Vat, third southern gallery,
"historic" bas-relief, Brahmins, (1st half 12th cent.)

CHAPTER V

TROUBLES IN THE 12TH CENTURY AND ADVENT OF JAYAVARMAN VII

1. Suryavarman II's successors

Between 1145, the last known date of Suryavarman II's reign, and 1181, date of the advent of Jayavarman VII, the Khmer kingdom experienced a troubled period of which we have, generally speaking, precious few details. We do not know the exact date of Suryavarman's death. It appears probable that it was sometime between 1150 and 1155. The Khmer embassy which was sent to China in 1155 may well correspond to the beginning of a new reign.

G. Coedès' hypothesis suggests a succession of four reigns after Suryavarman II's death: Dharanindravarman II, who reigned until approximately 1160, Yashovarman II, overthrown and put to death in 1165 by a usurper, Tribahuvanadityavarman, who was himself killed during the Cham invasion of 1177 and, finally, Jayavarman VII. Son of Dharanindravarman II, Jayavarman VII liberated Cambodia from the Cham occupation and was crowned in 1181. It seems surprising that Jayavarman VII did not succeed his father directly. G. Coedès advances that this apparently unusual succession can be explained by the fact that the prince was no doubt at war against the Chams at the time when Yashovarman II ascended to the throne. J. Boisselier, however, believes that Jayavarman VII had no reason to come to power in 1160, as he refutes the theory that Dharanindravarman II ever reigned in Cambodia.

2. Who was Dharanindravarman II ?

Let us quickly recapitulate the arguments advanced by J. Boisselier in order to remove Dharanindravarman II from the list of kings of Cambodia[20]. We know from the inscriptions ordered by Jayavarman VII that his father, Dharanindravarman II, was descended from the Mahidharapuras. A reading the inscriptions brings about an initial conclusion. Dharanindravarman appears in Jayavarman VII's genealogy, but he does not appear in the list of Suryavarman II's successors. In addition, Dharanindravarman II received no posthumous name. The divinity through which he is venerated is called Jayavarmasvaralokesha, "Lokesha, Lord of Jayavarman"; this is not a posthumous appellation of a sovereign but rather that of Jayavarman VII's guiding divinity. Finally, it is surprising that Jayavarman VII's mother and father were paid homage in separate temples, the first in Ta Prom, the second in Prah Khan. It is no less odd that the construction of Prah Khan, in honour of Dharanindravarman, was undertaken in 1191, ten years after Jayavarman VII's coronation, and five years after the construction of the foundation in honour of his mother. All becomes clear, however, when we notice that, in Jayavarman VII's panegyric, his mother's lineage was more powerful than his father's. Indeed, Jayavarman VII's mother, Princess Jayarajachudamani, was related to the most ancient of Khmer dynasties. Dharanindravarman was no doubt an individual of high rank, possessing sufficient power to obtain the right to a royal title, although it appears, as stated by J. Boisselier, that he was never king of Angkor.

Dharanindravarman was a devout Buddhist who, "honoured the feet of Jina (Buddha)". Jayavarman VII considered that is was the merits acquired from his father, which allowed him to be victorious over the Chams. It is for this reason that he paid him tribute in the form of the god "Jayavarmesvaralokesha".

3. Yashovarman II (?-1165)

Upon Suryavarman II's death, the kingdom probably found itself divided between a number of sovereigns. At the end of his reign, the king must have suffered defeats. He had placed a Khmer prince, his own brother-in-law in fact, on the throne of Vijaya in Champa; this prince was overthrown and killed. In the Menam basin, attacks on the city of Haripunjaya were cut short, and the kingdom of Lopburi declared their independence by sending an embassy to China in 1155. At the beginning of the second half of the 12th century, Cambodia experienced a little-known crisis.

We do not know the exact date of Yashovarman II's ascent to the throne, nor over which regions his power extended. It does appear certain that he lived in Angkor, but that his authority was disputed. An inscription at Banteay Chhmar tells us that Yashovarman II was attacked by an individual by the name of Bharata-Rahu. The king was saved by a young prince, Srindrakumara, who bears the title Rajakumara, "son of the king". It was thought that Srindrakuma was a child of Jayavarman VII, from whom emanates the inscription which describes this event. In this case, it would have to be admitted that Srindrakumara had attained his majority under the reign of Yashovarman II. He could have been the son of Jayavarman VII if this latter was born in 1125, but this seems too early. However, as J.M. Boisselier asserts, this Rajakumara may have been the son of Yashovarman II himself.

We do not know who Bharata-Rahu was, nor the reasons for his rebellion. His name recalls that of the asura Rahu who, during eclipses, attempts to devour the Sun and the Moon; this asura thus tries to take his revenge on the two divinities who had previously prevented him from stealing the nectar of everlasting life, come from the churning of the Sea of Milk. Rahu is therefore a dangerous and terrifying individual, whose name may well have been given to a rebel chief.

Yashovarman II's reign must have ended tragically. In 1165, a high dignitary overthrew him, had him put to death and inaugurated himself king, under the name of Tribhuvanadityavarman, "The One Whose Armour Is the Sun of the Three Worlds".

We do not know whether Yashovarman II undertook any construction in Angkor. It is possible that certain temples, which are associated with the style of Angkor Vat, were built or finished during his reign, either in the capital or in the provinces.

4. Usurpation of Tribhuvanadityavarman

Tribhuvanadityavarman reigned at Angkor for twelve years. We do not know how his usurpation was greeted. The inscription at Phimeanakas tells us, however, that the future Jayavarman VII, who was engaged in military operations against Champa at the time, returned hastily to Cambodia upon hearing of the Tribhuvanadityavarman rebellion. But, "Yashovarman, having been stripped of his royalty, Jayavarman remained in Cambodia waiting for the propitious moment to save the land rife with crime."

Did Jayavarman live in Angkor, or did he take refuge on his estate in Mahidharapura? The second hypothesis appears the most plausible, at it is highly unlikely that he was in the capital at the time of the tragic events of 1177.

5. Siege of Angkor by the Chams (1177)

One or two years after the violent overthrow of power by Tribhuvanadityavarman, the Champa instigated a second usurpation under Jaya Indravarman IV. This sovereign brought the war right into the heart of

Cambodia: "Jaya Indravarman, as presumptuous as Ravana[21], transporting his armies on carts, came like the sky to battle the nation of Kambu". Incapable of attaining the capital, Jaya Indravarman changed tactics; after having brought his army in by cart, he transferred them to junks. He took as his guide a shipwrecked China man, who knew the maritime routes well. In 1177, the Cham fleet followed the coast of present day Vietnam, ascended the Mekong across the delta, at came to the Great Lake at the mouth of the Siem Reap river. Angkor had no way of defending itself. Since its foundation, the city had never been threatened by a siege. Yashovarman's ramparts must have been time-worn; they did not even completely surround the city whose political and religious centre had developed around the Royal Palace. Only the temple of Angkor Vat had walls and moats. It is certain, however, that the surrounding walls of Angkor Vat, like its moats, were not conceived as a means of fortification. Yashodharapura's protection was not military but rather religious. Since Yassovaraman I, Khmer kings toiled to place Angkor in a divine world which was supposed to be invulnerable. So the city was siezed, in spite of divine protection. Disaster was complete. The Chams took over Angkor and pillaged it. Tribhuvanadityavarman was killed during an atrocious battle. The inscription says of the king of the Chams,

"in a battle made painful by Yama[22], who dwells in the southern region, and softened by the sun (having managed) to capture the king (of Cambodia) charged with the full scope (of his acts), killed him[23] ".

6. Consequences of the Cham victory

For some four years, the Chams settled in as masters of Angkor. The religious system which Yashovarman I and his successors had edified was invalidated.

What became of Angkor during these four years of Cham occupation? The pillage affected not only the Royal Treasury, but also the people's property. The protective gods of Angkor were no doubt transported to Champa, or mutilated, thus being robbed of their power. The city was not destroyed, however.

Jaya Indravarman's goal had been to have the Khmer kingdom at his mercy. A Chinese text emphasizes the implacability of the Chams crushing of Cambodia, thus:

The king of the Chams "assailed the capital of Chen-La by surprise with a mighty fleet, pillaged it and killed the king of Chen-La[24] without listening to any proposals for peace. From there was born a profound hatred which bore its fruit in a fifth of the armies of K'ing-yuan (1199)[25] ".

This "profound hatred" would indeed give birth to the liberation movement led by the future Jayavarman VII, and which would bring about the fall of Champa at the end of the century.

7. Cambodia's liberation by Jayavarman VII

We do not know how Jayavarman prepared his over-throw of the invaders. From a religious perspective, which is that of the inscriptions, the military organization of this coup is much less important than its merits, accumulated with the same goal in mind, but by relatives of the king. This is why the great stele of Phimeanakas[26] gives such a long description of the austerities practiced by Jayavarman VII's first queen, Jayarajadevi. "By her extreme devotion to her spouse... this good and divine princess desired see him pull the land out of this sea of misfortune in which it was plunged." This same text briefly recounts the battle led by Jayavarman VII:

> stanza LXX
> "Having, through his patience during misfortune, vanquished in combat this (king of the Chams) whose soldiers were like an ocean without shores, after having being crowned king, he possessed, through the conquest of Vijaya and other countries, a purified land which he could call home."

We have no more details on the military operations of this manoeuvre. It appears that a major battle was fought on the site of Prah Khan, to the north of Angkor. The decisive struggle was, no doubt, a naval battle which is depicted in two bas-reliefs, one at Banteay Chhmar, the other at Bayon. This latter is the larger of the two, as it covers an entire wall of one of the temple's galleries. Khmer and Cham vessels are locked in battle in many of the scenes. On the vessels' bridge, warriors prepare to attack; we recognize the Khmers from their bare heads and their brush cuts; the Chams by their strange helmets in the shape of upside-down flowers. The ships' hulls ram into one another. A hand to hand combat breaks out, the wounded and the dead fall into the water, where hungry crocodiles await them. On the upper registers is depicted a battle on land. Above the bas-relief, under an awning, the king himself oversees the operations and witnesses his enemies' defeat[27].

Below the battle, the sculptors have represented, in the form of a fresco, the daily life of the Khmer, the houses, market and activities which would be able to continue in an Angkor liberated by the victory of Jayavarman VII.

The date of Jayavarman VII's victory is not specified. It must, obviously, be before 1181 as this is the date of his coronation, a ceremony which would not have taken place before the full retreat of the Chams and the, at least partial, restoration of Angkor, since the city had been pillaged and its sanctuaries had been robbed of their precious images and wealth. Yashodharapura's reconstruction, which was as much religious as material, was the overwhelming task which befell Jayavarman VII; the king had first to complete his victory over the enemy in order to ensure that they would not return.

The battle against the Champa was long, painful and ruthless. Jayavarman VII was determined to carry through to the end; the Chinese author, Ma Tuan Lin, recalls that the sovereign had "vowed to extract an explosive vengeance from his enemies, which he achieved after eighteen patient years in hiding." In 1190, a new attack by the Chams re-ignited hostilities. An inscription in the Cham temple of Po Nagar in Nha Trang tells of Khmer troupes overthrowing the capital of Champa, and seizing all the linga. The Cham king was imprisoned in Cambodia and his country was divided into two kingdoms. Jayavarman placed one of his brothers-in-law and a Cham prince, who appears to have been owed a favour, on the thrones. Countering this latter prince's revolt required military intervention once again and, in 1203, Jayavarman VII reduced Champa to a single Khmer province.

It was not enough to guard against renewed attack from the Chams; it was necessary to arm Cambodia once and for all against a disaster such as the one which had brought it to its knees in 1177. In taking Angkor, the Chams proved that the city was not invulnerable, even if it was thought to be the divine kingdom on earth. It became essential to find a protection superior to that which had been established over the previous centuries. This was, without a doubt, one of Jayavarman VII's principal preoccupations. He rebuilt Angkor while investing it with a symbolism which was far richer than the one which his predecessors had established.

1 Statue presumed to be of King Jayavarman VII
(National Museum of Phnom Penh), Bayon style,
(end 12th-early 13th cent.)

2 Prah Khan of Angkor, stature
of Queen Jayarajadevi, wife of Jayavarman VII
(in place) , Bayon style, (end 12th-early 13th cent.)

3 Temple of Banteay Kdei, (end 12th cent.)

4 Sanctuary and the centre of the Neak-Pean basin, view from the east, and drafted statue of the horse Balaha, (end 12th-early 13th cent.)

CHAPTER VI

JAYAVARMAN VII
AND THE EDIFICATION OF ANGKOR THOM

1. King Jayavarman VII (1181-1218?)

Jayavarman VII was the son of Dharanindravarman, who was probably a local king, and of Jayarajachudamani, descendant of the Sreshthapura lineage who had once ruled in Chen-La. It was through his mother that he obtained his rights to the throne. Speaking at once of his "brilliant power" and of his great abilities as chief warrior, the inscription of Prah Khan emphasizes his moral and intellectual qualities: "devoted to goodness, having his conscience raised by the increase of virtues, talented... worthy of his masters' respect, he was considered to be a veritable Panini[28], from a very young age."

The inscriptions depict him as hero and wise man. It was sometimes said that he was given to excessive fervour, and has even been accused of hypocrisy. Jayavarman VII's personality is far more complex, however. His talents as politician and warrior are undeniable. Ma Tuan-Lin describes him as " waiting patiently", which can hardly be construed as hypocrisy. Having returned from Champa at the time when the usurpers were firmly implanted in

Cambodia, it is likely that he took refuge in his property; struggling perhaps to refrain from action, but having sufficient self-control and a sense of timing to not expend his forces uselessly, but rather to gather them in order to act at the most propitious moment. There exist a number of statues which appear to be portraits of Jayavarman VII; all depict the king in a meditative posture, devoid of all royal attributes. One of these statues was found at Krol Romeas, to the north of Angkor Thom; all show a thick-set man whose hair is either short or gathered up in a small bun at the crown. The expression is one of profound meditation.

We know, from the large stele at Phimeanakas, that Jayavarman VII's first wife was Jayarajadevi; it contains a lengthy panegyric, composed in her honour by her sister, Indradevi:

Fervent Buddhist, she was given to severe austerity, while her spouse was engaged in battle against the Chams, first in a far off land, and then on Cambodian soil. The text describes her as, "consumed by asceticism, thinned by devotion". Finally, "having rejoined her spouse, the king of kings, out of gratitude, she (let fall) a shower of magnificent gifts (upon the earth)." The queen's happiness must have been short-lived, as she died not long after the king's coronation. Jayavarman VII thus attributed the rank of first queen to Indradevi, "intelligent by nature, scholarly and very pure".

2. Jayavarman VII's religious concepts

The son of Dharanindravarman, who found satisfaction in the nectar of the religion of Sakyamuni, Jayavarman VII was a devout Buddhist. His religious attitude is reflected in his concept of royal power and of the duties which such influence imposes on the sovereign. Jayavarman VII's ideal was that of the Shakravartin monarch, the Indian king Ashoka. He too wished to be a Shakravartin sovereign perhaps, in part, out of a taste for power but, above all, because the kingdom would be blessed with prosperity and stability under such a monarch.

After having chased the Chams from Cambodia, Jayavarman VII confirmed his power in the Menam basin and in southern Laos, where a Khmer inscription dating from his reign was found at Say Fong, near Vientian. The monarch knew that a fallen kingdom could rise again, as had Cambodia under his hand. He wanted to give his country indestructible protection. In reproducing Mount Meru in the capital, his predecessors had thought they were establishing the divine world at the heart of their kingdom. Their hope was obliterated by the invasion of 1177[29] . Jayavarman VII therefore had the task of establishing a far superior religious defense. It is no doubt for this reason that he erected such a large number of temples and monasteries throughout the land, and especially in the Angkor region.

3. The great foundations

During Jayavarman VII's reign, great foundations sprung up around the capital. The first was probably that of Banteay Kdei, then Ta Prohm, in 1186, and, in 1191, the Prah Khan group. There were other charitable foundations and lesser temples: Ta Nei, Krol Ko, Banteay Prei, Ta Som, to name but a few. The city of Angkor Thom itself was rebuilt and surrounded by a fortifying wall. The central temple of the capital restored, Bayon was edified, no doubt in the second part of the reign.

In the provinces, temples were built throughout the kingdom, from the Menam basin to the shores of the Mekong, and from lower Laos to the southern regions of Cambodia. The most remarkable of these provincial temples which may be attributed to Jayavarman VII is without a doubt Banteay Chhmar.

In as far as we can tell, these temples have complex layouts. With the exception of Bayon, they are not set on raised bases. The enclosures, walls or galleries, are pierced with gopura. These latter were highly developed and were sometimes linked by rooms which were subsequently hastily decorated. The gopura opened onto passages which converge toward the central sanctuary. Annex temples, which may be surrounded by galleries, sometimes overlap inside the monument.

Many of the temples built during Jayavarman VII's reign contain sanctuaries or gopura adorned with four-faced towers. This characteristic existed at no other time. Many have surmised as to the significance of the faces on these towers. J. Boisselier notes that they do not always depict the same divinity. In studying Jayavarman VII's foundations briefly, we are led to conclude that the aspect of the faces on these towers differs according to the buildings which they adorn. It is evident that the four-faced tower which top the outer gopura at Banteay Kdei differ from those which may be seen on the doors of Angkor Thom. It is difficult to ascertain which divinities were honoured at Banteay Kdei as the monument's founding stele has not been found. The temple is, unfortunately, also in ruins. A vast body of water, the Srah Strang, or "Royal Bath", stretches out in front of the entrance to which one gains access by a splendid pier adorned with naga.

4. Ta Prohm

The Rajavihara, or "Royal Monastery", which is now known as Ta Prohm, or "Old Brahma", was founded in 1186 in honour of Jayavarman VII's mother and guru. The deceased princess was presented as Prajnaparamita, "Perfect Wisdom", the mystic mother of all Buddhas.

A characteristic of Ta Prohm proves that this monument had been a monastery; the layout contains stone cells for the monks. The entire surface of the central sanctuary was hammered in preparation for a layer of coating.

Between the third and fourth enclosures opens out a grand park, measuring some sixty hectares. It is there that the temple's personnel, 12,640 people according to the ins- criptions, must have dwelled. The stone cells could have housed only a small number of monks. The personnel must have lived in wooden houses. In addition to the eigh- teen grand priests and 2,740 officiants, 2,232 assistants were assigned to the temple. Living in the Rajavihara, then, we find a population equal to that of a small town. The monastery possessed great wealth and received its funds from the 3,140 surrounding villages.

5. Prah Khan

The outer walls of Prah Khan comprise a rectangle of 700 metres by 800 metres. They surrounded a veritable city founded upon the site at which Jayavarman VII marked his victory over the Chams. The inscription of Prah Khan celebrates the creation of this city which bears the name of Jayasri, the "Fortune of Victory":

stanza XXXII,
"At the place where, during the battle, receptacle of the enemy's blood, he had been victorious (Jayasri), he founded a village with this same name (Jayasri), whose stones and golden lotus change the colour of the floor, which still shines today as though covered in blood."

The current name of Prah Khan designates the Sacred Sword, housed in the Royal Palace of Phnom Penh, which was considered the kingdom's palladium.

One gains access to Prah Khan by four roads bordered by two giant rows on stones supporting a naga. This access road recalls the one at Angkor Thom and, like Angkor Thom, Prah Khan is not only a temple, but also a city. To the east and to the west, the roads are preceded by a path bordered by stone markers.

In the temple, Jayavarman VII consecrated a statue of his father, in 1191, represented as Lokesvara[30]; it is this image which is a "Lokesha named Sri Jayavarmesvara'", Jayavarman's god of predilection. Representations of Lokesvara dating from this era are numerous as devotion to this compassionate Bodhisattva was extremely widespread. In the sanctuaries and on the temple pediments, one finds recognizable images of the Buddha Amitabha, "Infinite Brightness", which Lokesvara wears in his hair. Around the Jayavarmesvaralokesha, 283 images of the gods were erected. Among the four principal gods, Sri Yassovarmesvara and Sri Tribhuvanavarmesvara recall Jayavarman VII's predecessors. In the area around the central sanctuary, in the courtyard surrounded by the gallery of the first enclosure, more than twenty tiny sanctuaries, which G. Coedès called "family tombs", were built in memory of the dead.

The inscription enumerates the donations which must be made each day to the divinities of Prah Khan, beginning with Lokesvara. These offerings consisted of rice, sesame, peas, melted butter, curdled milk, fresh milk, molasses and oil. In the same text we find a list of fabrics to be offered as clothing for the statues: white and red flannel for clothes and "Chinese silk veils to protect Lokesvara and the other gods' feet from mosquitoes". The inscription also mentions the offerings to be made to the temple's personnel; they consist of the same products to be offered to the gods, but in much larger quantities; the personnel was numerous, sometimes in the tens of thousands.

6. Neak Pean

The stele of Prah Khan mentions a certain number of sanctuaries, many of which are difficult to place. One of them, on the other hand, is easily identifiable, namely that of the Isle of Rajyasri; it corresponds to the monument of Neak Pean, or "coiled naga". It rises up in the centre of Jayatataka basin, which the inscription describes as "a lucky mirror, coloured by stones, gold and garlands". Neak Pean contains a prasat supported by a lotus resting on a base; two naga are coiled around this base, hence the name. The fairly deep, square basin is surrounded by sandstone covered grades. The pavilions were built on the basin's edge for ablutions; they receive the water from gargoyles in the shape of a male head, to the east, of a lion to the south, of a horse to the west and of an elephant to the north. After having crossed through the pavilion of ablution, the water falls into four basins which have been dug on the four sides of the main body of water.

In 1923, L. Finot and V. Goubev recognized the fact that Neak Pean was a replica of Lake Anavatapa, the sacred mythical site of the Himalayas[31]. From the lake four rivers flow out, one toward each of the cardinal points. J. Boisselier reinstigated the study of Neak Pean based on the Prah Kahn stele as well as on various texts regarding Lake Anavatapta[32]. He demonstrated the importance of Neak Pean in terms of the symbolism of the capital and its surrounding regions. We will confine ourselves to citing only a few of Boisselier's conclusions. According to Indian texts, the waters of Lake Anavatapta are always cool as they are never hit with direct sunlight, but rather by reflected light. The inscription at Prah Khan states that the pond at Neak Pean "is lit by the light of the golden prasada", hence not by direct sunlight. In Buddhist cosmology, Lake Anavatapta will be the last lake to dry up at the end of time; the kingdom which possesses it is therefore guaranteed to exist an equally long time in the present world. Moreover, the lake's water is considered holy; during the coronation of a Shakravartin king, the sovereign must be anointed with water drawn from Lake Anavatapta. J. Boisselier notes that the "foundation has a dual task for Cambodia: it guarantees the kingdom's perpetuity as well as assuring its sovereign's universality." In the basin which surrounds the existing sanctuary, we find vestiges of four sculptures in the round. To the south, there are stone fragments which are impossible to identify whereas, to the east, there are fragments of a Vishnu in a state of repose; to the north we make out a linga. Finally, to the east, the image of the famous horse, Balaha, was reconstituted.

This marvellous horse is the aspect taken on by Lokesvara in order to save victims of a shipwreck who had washed up on the island of an ogresses and, on the verge of being devoured, had invoked this compassionate Bodhisattva[33].

There is nothing surprising in the image of the Balaha swimming toward the sanctuary where Lokesvara is to be found, and towing the victims who cling to his flanks. On the contrary, it is somewhat surprising to see two Brahminic gods depicted in a basin which represents Lake Anavatapta. The Prah Khan stele says that Jayavarman VII had placed 14 gods, "on the isle of Jayasri of a thousand lingas". On this same subject, P. Mus had already stated that it would have been an intelligent gesture to group around Buddha the cults which had guaranteed Cambodia's power since the origins of the Angkoran monarchy, but which had been overthrown during the Cham incursion in 1177. J. Boisselier believes that it was essential to revive the ancient cults by presenting them in a new light. It was his opinion that the presence of the Brahminic gods around

Buddha fully sanctifies Rajyasri, and contributes to the
creation of the basin, "the most eminent site, heightening
the symbolism, even of Anavatapta itself which, being the
home of the gods, will escape world destruction..."

7. The surrounding area of Angkor Thom:
hospital chapels and rest huts

Angkor Thom was the heart of the country; it was there
that all routes which led to the outermost regions conver-
ged. The roads were pious deeds which Jayavarman VII
sanctified by lining them with rest huts and hospitals[34].
Certain of these pious establishments could be found on
the outskirts of Angkor Thom itself.

The hospitals founded by Jayavarman VII numbered in
the two hundred. The buildings which were made of perishable materials have long since been destroyed, but the
sites upon which they were built sometimes still contain a
chapel and a founding stele. The texts of the "hospital stelae" are almost all identical. Four hospital chapels were
found around Angkor Thom: to the east, the "Hospital
Chapel" near Ta Keo; to the south, the Ta Prohm Kel; to the
west, a chapel which bears no particular name; and, to the
north, the discovery of a stele allowed for the identification, around 1954, of the Prasat Tonle Sngout as a hospital chapel. The stele state that these chapels and the hospitals themselves were dedicated to Buddha Bhaishajyaguru
Vaiduryaprabha, the "Master of remedies who possesses
the brilliance of beryl". Doctors and personnel were affilia-
ted with these hospitals, as were two sacrificers and one

astrologer. The text of the inscription enumerates all of the medication which was to be provided for the establishment. The sick from "the four castes" could be treated in these hospitals.

According to the stele of Prah Khan, Jayavarman VII built 121 rest huts, or "houses with fire", along the roads wherein pilgrims or travellers could stop for rest and relaxation. A few sanctuaries belonging to these establishments still remain. They were comprised of a cella preceded by a long antechamber. Rest huts were built within the walls of many of the larger temples and monasteries, and may still be seen at Ta Prohm and Prah Khan, for example.

8. Inside Angkor Thom

The city of Yassodharpura was seized by the Chams in 1177, but was neither burned nor destroyed. Jayavarman VII's city does not coincide with that of Yashovarman, however; it is less spread out as well as being situated farther north. Its centre is the Bayon temple.

Angkor's ramparts mark out a square measuring three kilometres on either side. Made of laterite, they lean against earthen mounds, and are surrounded by a 100 metre-wide moat. Five doors allow access through the walls, one each on the northern, southern and western faces, and two on the eastern face: The Gate of the Dead and the Victory Gate. A road intesects the moat at each point of entry. At each corner rise small temples, the Prasat Chrung.

In the inscriptions of the Prasat Chrung, it is said that Jayavarman VII founded a "Jayagiri (mountain of victory) whose peak scraped the sky" and "a Jyasindhu (ocean of victory) whose immeasurable depths touched the serpents' world". Thus the enclosure of Angkor Thom is much more than merely fortifications, it is also rife with symbolism: the wall is the mountain chain which surrounds the universe, the moat is the cosmic ocean containing the eight naga which hold up the world.

In front of the doors, the roads which cross over the moat are bordered by two rows of giants supporting a naga. Anyone entering the city sees, to the left, gentle-faced giants crowned with the tiara of the gods and, to the right, creatures with globular eyes and whose hairstyle is that of a warrior, adorned with leaves. The giants seem to be preventing the naga from fleeing. G. Coedès sees, in the naga, a representation of Indra's bow, the rainbow which links the world of man with the world of the gods. In the doorway corners, we find Indra himself in relief, mounted on his three-headed elephant.

The doors of Angkor Thom are topped with four faces. J. Boisselier noted[35] that four distinct heads are represented, as opposed to one head with four faces; he believes that this is a depiction of the four divinities ruling over the four directions.

The architectural style of these doorways is of an admirable majesty; in front of each of these high, slim doors lay two rows of massive and powerful giants.

9. Bayon

Bayon, the central temple of Angkor Thom, is perhaps the most characteristic monument of Jayavarman VII's era. Its construction no doubt began during the second half of his reign. Its unusual design contains no enclosure; its walls were the walls of the city. The capital was therefore contained within the holy walls. Bayon consists mainly of a complex of sanctuaries, in the shape of a raised massif, surrounded by two galleries whose walls are covered with bas-reliefs. The central sanctuary is a cella, encircled by a walkway and sixteen surrounding chapels which open up to the outside. The peculiar style of this circular layout forms a sort of yantra, or magic diagramme. Other sanctuaries are placed around the central massif. At first glance, this body of buildings give a mysterious and odd impression. The sanctuaries have four monumental faces in their super-structures. P. Stern demonstrated that the towers topped with faces appear only in the second movement of the style to which Bayon gave its name, hence during the second part of Jayavarman VII's reign. The deterioration of the superstructures of the central massif makes it impossible to establish the exact layout of the faces in the upper section.

There has been much conjecture regarding the significance of the towers of sculpted faces. P. Mus thought[36] that they represented the Bodhisattva Lokesvara Samantamukha, "Lokesvara who has faces in every direction". J. Boisselier pointed out, however, that the faces on the towers of Bayon are crowned with diadems decorated with leaves, a style which is reserved for warriors, and which would not have been worn by Lokesvara. He suggested that these colossal images were Brahma Sanankumara, or "forever young", who had come to sit by each one of the gods. Bayon would then correspond to the Assembly hall of the gods in Indra's city, honoured by Buddha's presence[37] .

Bayon's central sanctuary is dedicated to Buddha. In 1933, a very large statue of Buddha protected by the naga was found under the central sanctuary. The inscriptions sculpted in the entrance to the radiating chapels allowed for the discovery of the fact that they were dedicated to familial royal and provincial cults. This is why G. Coedès wrote, "in the same manner in which the city's enclosure and central mountain constituted a reduced model of the universe, Bayon represented the kingdom."

10. The Royal Palace and Angkor Thom's Great Square

The dwelling places of the palace have disappeared although it is still possible to see two basins near the Royal Palace, one of which is embellished with sculptures in the Bayon style. On the upper registers of these sculptures we find rows of male and female garuda[38] and, on the lower grades, mythical fish and sea creatures.

Before the enclosure and the gopura which were erected at the end of the 10th century, a large east-facing terrace measuring over 300 metres, known as the "Elephants' Terrace", was built. One may gain access to it by enormous perrons in the centre and at either end. On either side of the central perron, on the wall covered with sculpted bas-reliefs, we find alternating lions and Atlas-like garuda. On the walls which extend beyond the central perrons, to the north and south, we find a long line of elephants, some of which are locked in battle with savage beasts.

To the north of the Elephants' Terrace rises the "Terrace of the Leper King", whose dual facing is covered with characters laid out in register. Recent clearings have allowed us to uncover the development of the northern part of this terrace. The construction owes its name to the statue of a figure who is arbitrarily known as the "Leper King". This image was certainly never that of a real leper; it is more likely to be an as yet unidentified divinity. This "Leper King", which is by no means one of the most beautiful sculptures of the day, has fangs at the corner of his mouth; it could therefore be a god of death or of the underworld.

11. End of Jayavarman VII's reign

The last embassy sent to China by Jayavarman VII was in the year 1200, although nothing proves that the king did not survive long after this date. It is possible that he reigned until 1218. The diminishing of Cambodian power, to the east and west, around 1220 may be a consequence of his death, the exact date of which is absent from the texts.

One of Jayavarman VII's sons succeeded him, under the name of Indravarman II. The epigraphy renders us the names of several of the great king's sons, but nothing allows us to ascertain which one of them ascended to the throne upon his death.

The body of work left by Jayavarman VII is considerable. His name will be forever associated not only with Angkor Thom and Bayon but also with many sanctuaries, notably the temple city of Prah Khan and the Ta Prohm monastery. These edifices are but a part of this sovereign's works. It bears monumental witness to the political and religious organization of the Khmer kingdom, and should not be perceived as a group of buildings erected feverishly by a megalomaniac king. Rich in symbolism, these monuments were meant to make of Cambodia an unshakable kingdom.

Jayavarman VII's hopes were to be dashed, "Even if all of the buildings which were to bestow indisputable power on Cambodia were to crumble within 250 years, this was not the case of the system whose goal was to materialize the Shakravartin's power, and to associate royal Hindu rites with the practice of Buddhism... a system which survives not only in Cambodia, but which is still espoused by numerous Buddhist kingdoms in South-East Asia.[39]"

In the capital, overrun by forest, the monuments erected by Jayavarman VII survive within a religious atmosphere. A slight smile lights the faces of the temple's gods and guardian devata, as do the faces sculpted in the superstructures of the prasat. On the statues which are presumed to be of Jayavarman VII, the "smile of Bayon", full of Buddhist compassion, softens the features of this king who sports no symbols of royal glory.

1 Angkor Thom, south door, (end 12th cent.)

2 Bayon, Central temple of Angkor Thom,
view from the east, (end 12th-early 13th cent.)

3 Bayon, north-east corner, tower of four faces
(end 12th-early 13th cent.)

4 Bayon, devata, (end 12th-early 13th cent.)

CHAPTER VII

ANGKOR AND ANGKORAN SOCIETY DURING THE 13TH CENTURY

1. Jayavarman VII's first successors

The years following the death of Jayavarman VII were marked by a diminishing of Khmer power in Champa, as well as in the Menam basin which consisted of Thai principalities. In the second half of the 13th century, King Mangray dominated northern Thailand, while Rama K'amheng founded the kingdom of Sudhodaya in the centre of the Menam basin.

We know little of the reign of Indravarman II, who died in 1243. After him, Jayavarman VIII ruled Cambodia. Nothing tells us how these two men were related. It is probable that it was Jayavarman VIII who faced the first Siamo-Khmer war following Rama K'amheng's conquest of the former Cambodian provinces.

It was during Jayavarman VIII's reign that the Mangalartha, the last sandstone temple, was built in Angkor. Jayavarman VIII erected this temple in 1295 in honour of Jayamangalartha, the cousin of one of his spouses' who was the daughter of a Burmese brahmin.

Jayavarman VIII was a Hindu, as is confirmed by his posthumous name, Paramesvarapada. It seems likely that, under his reign, acts of violence against Buddhist representations were committed. On the pediments, the markers and the pillars of Jayavarman VII's sanctuaries, the images of Buddha were felled. The images of Lokesvara were not smashed, but the small Buddhas which they wore in their hair were removed, as were the objects which they held in their hands.

During the 13th century, Singalese Buddhism began to spread throughout Cambodia. The stay of one of Jayavarman VII's sons in Ceylon marked the beginning of this new religious orientation. Up until then, Cambodia had practiced Mahayana[40] Buddhism, whose texts are written almost exclusively in Sanskrit. With the 13th century came the development of Theravada[41] Buddhism, whose canonical texts were written in Pali. The Theravada would be adopted in Cambodia, as well as in Thailand and Laos where it remains the state religion to this day.

Jayavarman VIII must have been quite elderly in 1295. One inscription mentions that "the earth sustained by an old king felt the discomfort of an abundance of thorns." The country was no doubt divided, "sheltered under a crowd of the king's white parasols". Jayavarman VIII abdicated in favour of his son-in-law, Srindravarman. Chiu Ta-Kuan, a China man come to Cambodia in 1296, tells of this abdication, which appears to have been the result of a revolution in the palace. His account is dramatic:

"The new prince is the son-in-law of the former; he adopted the career of arms. The father-in-law loved his daughter; the daughter stripped him of the golden sword and handed it to her husband. The son, robbed of his succession, plotted to rally the troops. The new prince learned of the subterfuge, cut off his toes and relegated him to a dark chamber. The new prince's body is clad in iron... it is only because of this precaution that he dares to go out."[42]

It appears that Srindravarman re-established order, placing the earth "in the shade of a single white parasol".

2. The voyage of Chiu Ta-Kuan

In the year following the abdication of Jayavarman VIII, a Chinese embassy was sent to Cambodia. Among the ambassador's entourage was Chiu Ta-Kuan who, upon his return to China, wrote his memoirs on Cambodian customs[43]. In this text, he recounts what he saw, or heard tell, during his stay. He opens the doors to the Angkor of the late 13th century, at a time when the capital was at the height of its glory, having not yet been victims of the Siamese invasions. The glory of the monarchy evidently impressed this Chinese traveller. The people's habits at once astonished, amused and sometimes shocked him.

It must be noted that Chiu Ta-Kuan often saw Cambodian life through the eyes of his countrymen who had settled in Angkor. Certain Chinese had been living in Cambodia for a long time. They apparently lived very well as, according to Chiu Ta-Kuan:

"Rice is easy to earn, women are easy to find, houses are easy to set up, furniture is easy to find, business is easy to run. There are always many who come to settle in this country."

Chiu Ta-Kuan does say, however, that he stayed with a Cambodian family; he was therefore able to observe much of what he recounted. His description of Angkor corresponds well to what we may still witness nowadays. Many of his notations can be confirmed through the scenes depicted in the bas-reliefs of Bayon, or by information given in the inscriptions.

3. The city's monumental aspect

Chiu Ta-Kuan's description of Angkor allows us to recognize Angkor Vat, the walls and doors of Angkor Thom, the temples of Bayon and Baphuon; while now all that is left are the ruins of all these edifices, this Chinese traveller had the privilege of penetrating into the living city. We arrive at Angkor with him, follow the roadway bordered by stone giants holding back the two naga, and we go through the door crowned with faces. Current access opens wide onto a forest path.

Chiu Ta-Kuan saw "the large doors, closed at night, open in the morning" and the "guards at the entrance, which only dogs may not pass through". Also excluded from the capital were "criminals whose toes had been chopped off".

Wandering through the city's streets, the Chinese traveller had the opportunity to admire the houses of the princes and high officers, all facing east, partly covered by tile roofs, whereas the outbuildings had roofs of straw. The bas-reliefs of Bayon depict these same dwellings, covered with round tiles. While in the outbuildings the domestics worked, inside opulent houses the rich lived easily. The splendour of the nobles' houses marks a contrast to the cottages found in the more modest neighbourhoods and villages.

Chiu Ta-Kuan saw the grand temples. He recounts that at Bayon:

"Marking the centre of the kingdom, it has a gold tower, flanked by over twenty stone towers, and hundreds of stone cells. On the east side are a golden bridge and a golden lion on either side of the bridge."

Indeed, to the east, one gains access to Bayon by a large terrace resting on columns which allows one to cross the moat; a lion is placed on either side of the path of access.

"At approximately one Ii to the north of the golden tower, there is a copper tower which is even higher than the golden one, and which offers a truly impressive view."

The copper tower was probably Baphuon, whose inner sanctuary Chiu Ta-Kuan may have seen but which we are left only to imagine.

4. The Royal Palace

Finally, the Chinese chronicler arrived at the Royal Palace and its temple, the Phimeanakas. In front of the Royal Palace, bordering the Great Square of Angkor Thom, stretches out the Elephants' Terrace which support light constructions. These buildings have disappeared, but Chiu Ta-Kuan saw them; the Council Chamber was perhaps situated there, supported by the elephants. This Council Chamber must have been magnificent, with its square, mirrored columns and "golden" window frames.

"I heard tell that inside the Palace there were many marvellous spots; but the protection is very tight and it is impossible to enter."

It is therefore based on descriptions given to him that he is able to render the inside of this magnificent structure, its long verandahs and covered hallways, "solid and irregular, without much symmetry". Not having been able to enter the Royal Palace and to see the way in which people lived there, he listened to rumours which circulated among the common men regarding the king's residence. It is thus that he recounts how the king must climb, every night, to the "golden tower" in the palace, the Phimeanakas.

"All of the natives claim that inside the tower lives the soul of a nine-headed serpent, master of the earth of the entire kingdom. He appears every night in the

form of a woman. It is with him that the sovereign must
first couple... he leaves at the second watch, and may
then sleep with his wives and concubines. If, one night,
the serpent's soul does not appear, it means that the
king's end is nigh. If the sovereign misses a single night,
great misfortune will befall the kingdom."

The Chinese chronicler is more at ease in his descriptions of the royal audience which he was able to
attend when he accompanied his country's ambassador:

"The king holds open court twice each day, for the affairs of
government... Civil service or commoners who wish to see the
prince sit on the ground to wait for him. After a time, music is
heard from deep inside the palace, outside they blow a conch to
welcome the king... An instant later, we see two girls of the palace
raise a curtain with their tiny fingers, and the king, sword in hand,
appears at the golden window. Ministers and commoners alike
join hands and lower the foreheads to the ground. When the
sound of the conchs has ceased, they may raise their heads.
Following the king's good wishes, they approach and sit by him...
When the affairs have been concluded, the prince turns around;
the two girls of the palace lower the curtain; everyone rises."

It is thus that the king is presented, in the bas-reliefs,
in elegant pavilions, accompanied by the members of
his Court, receiving homage or the petitions of his prostrate subjects. Chiu Ta-Kuan was evidently impressed
by the ceremony. He concludes that the Cambodians,
"know how to recognize a prince".

The Chinese traveller describes the sovereign's
magnificent garb:

"Only the prince is allowed to wear tightly woven fabric. He is crowned by a gold diadem. When he is not wearing his diadem, he wraps garlands of fragrant, jasmine type, flowers around his chignon. From his neck hang close to three pounds of large beads. On his wrists, ankles and fingers, he wears bracelets and rings set with tiger's eyes. He goes barefoot, and the soles of his feet and the palms of his hands are dyed red by the red drug. When he goes out, he holds the golden sword in his hand."

5. Society

The social structure changed very little between the 11th and 13th centuries; in Chiu Ta-Kuan's account we find, however, a description of society which does not appear in the inscriptions. His account relates that Buddhists were given a greater role than Brahmins, whom he calls Pan-k'i. Being Chinese, he would have had little contact with the brahmins, although the sacerdotal caste does not seem to have lost any of its importance at that time, in spite of the growth of Theravada Buddhism.

Chiu Ta-Kuan admits his ignorance of the gods revered by the Brahmins, and of their sacred texts. He remarks that the Pan-k'i dress like other Khmers, although they wear the Brahminic white cotton belt, tied around their neck, and which must never be removed. He notes their importance in the social context as, says he, "the Pan-k'i who enter the service are given high positions". This notation coincides with the information revealed about the Brahmins' careers in the epigraphic texts.

The Chinese chronicler did not fail to mention the importance of the ministers and their hierarchy in the social structure:

"In this country, there are councilors, generals, astronomers, etc., and below them, all manner of inferior employees... Most of the time, princes are chosen for the positions; otherwise, the elected offer up their daughters as royal concubines. The insignias and the resulting attributions also depend on rank."

Beneath the privileged classes, Chiu Ta-Kuan mentions the commoners, "rude and very black. Whether they live in the far off villages of the isles in the sea, or in the busiest streets, they are all one." More humble still are the slaves:

"They buy savages to use as servants. Those who have many, have over a hundred; those who have few, have between ten and twenty. Only the very poor have none at all. The savages are men from the isolated mountain regions. They belong to a race of their own... They may only sit and sleep underneath the main floor. They may ascend in order to serve, but they must kneel, perform the anjali,[44] prostrate themselves, and then advance... If they commit an error, they are beaten, they lower their head and do not dare to move."

6. The people's activities

We know next to nothing of ordinary life in Angkor, before the end of the 12th century, since all of the information we have comes from the inscriptions which say nothing of the common man. On the other hand, from the end of the 12th to the end of the 13th century, the bas-reliefs, in addition to Chiu Ta-Kuan's chronicles, give us a wealth of information surrounding the everyday activities of ordinary Khmers. It is interesting to note that Chiu Ta-Kuan's notations correspond well with the images of the bas-reliefs at Bayon.

In the streets, the Chinese traveller saw carts covered with basket work, and pulled by oxen, people on horseback or riding in palanquins carried by two porters, as depicted in the bas-reliefs. Walking through the market, he saw men carrying goods which hung from either end of a yoke. He stopped by the stalls of small fish or fruit sellers. Perhaps he paused to watch a cock or pig fight, like the ones represented in the bas-reliefs of Bayon.

Commerce was one of the principal urban activities. Chiu Ta-Kuan says that it is in the hands of the women. The sellers' stands are extremely basic:

"They do not have permanent boutiques, but use a sort of straw mat placed on the ground. Everyone has his space. I heard tell that they paid rent on their space to a mandarin. The minor transactions are paid in rice, cereals, Chinese objects; next come sheets; larger transactions are paid for with gold and silver."

Peasants bring the products which they cultivate: onions, leeks, eggplants, watermelons, squash. During his walks through the city, the Chinese traveller watched the weavers at work, and examined the fabric imported from abroad:

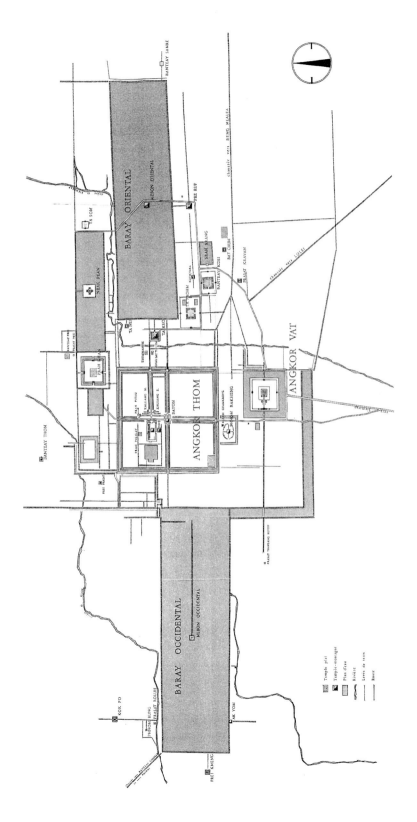

"There are many different qualities of fabric. The one worn by
the prince is worth two or three ounces of gold; they are the most
beautiful, both for their colour and their fineness. Although they
weave cotton, much is imported from Siam and Champa, and the
most highly regarded is that come from the Western seas, valued
for its fine craftsmanship."

Chiu Ta-Kuan was particularly interested in those
goods which his countrymen could buy in Cambodia:
ivory, king-fisher feathers, rhinoceros horns, beeswax,
cardamom, pepper and resin.

7. Private Life

Although foreigners were excluded from the events
of Cambodian private life, Chiu Ta-Kuan was able to
recount a number of customs which he was able to
observe while living with a Khmer family, or which he
heard of from his, more or less well informed, compa-
triots.

Entering modest houses, he was able to see the spar-
se furnishings, often consisting of a couple of jars set on
the ground, a few baskets hanging from the rafters,
cauldrons and earthen ovens. These utensils can be
seen depicted in the villagers' houses, underneath the
scene of the great naval battle, in the southern gallery
of Bayon; but we may also see them in the current day
market places of Phnom Penh or Kompong Chhnang,
the "Port of Cauldrons". Sometimes the materials are
simpler still:

"The people of the average class have a house but no table, bench, basin or pail. In order to cook the rice, they use an earthen pot; to prepare the sauce, they use an earthen pan. They bury three stones to make their fireplace, and use a coconut as a ladle. To serve the rice, they use Chinese earthenware or copper plates. For the sauce they use leaves from the trees which serve as small cups which, when filled with juice, do not leak."

The noblemen's houses contain a much richer decor:

"The houses of the rich and noble sometimes use silver, and even gold, recipients. In this country, gold dishes are used for birthdays... Straw mats are laid on the ground... or tiger, panther or deer skins, or wicker mats. They have recently adopted low tables, measuring about one foot high. For sleeping, they use only straw mats laid on the wooden floor. Some have very recently begun to sleep on low beds which are generally made by the Chinese."

The Khmers are clad in either fine or heavy fabric, according to their wealth. Their clothes, as described by Chiu Ta-Kuan, correspond to those seen in the sculptures. "Women and men alike wear only a piece of fabric around the hips", leaving their chest bare. "When they go out, they add a large strip of cotton which they drape over the small one." They go barefoot. Their hair is done up in a bun. The Chinese traveller notes that, "the common women have no adornment in their hair, but they do wear gold rings and bracelets."

Chiu Ta-Kuan tells us little about the private religious ceremonies which are linked to the important everyday events: birth, marriage and death. He speaks of the deflowering of nubile girls and of the abandonment of cadavers to vultures and dogs.

8. Festivities

Among the annual festivities, the most important seems to be New Year's, welcomed in with rockets and firecrackers. A nautical festival, which takes place during the fifth month, may have a rapport with the Water Festival which, nowadays, marks the end of the rainy season, and the reversal of the tide of the Tonle Sap. To these, Chiu Ta-Kuan adds the festival of the rice harvest, a ceremony in which the statues of Buddha are anointed.

The celebration of these festivals by the king evoke festivities which have been maintained at the Court of Phnom Penh, up until this day: "in front of the palace, a large rostrum is raised and decorated with lanterns and flowers"; "everyone begs the king to come and watch the spectacle". Everyone takes part in the festival for which the Mandarins and noblemen spend considerable amounts. Finally, "the sovereign invites the foreign ambassadors to the spectacle."

Sometimes sumptuous processions paraded through the streets of the capital, when the king "went to see a small golden pagoda, in front of which is a gold Buddha". Chiu Ta-Kuan describes this procession, led by horsemen, banners, flags and music, rather complacently:

The women of the Court number more than three thousand girls holding candles, gold and silver utensils, and an entire regiment of young girls armed with a sword and shield. The ministers, princes, the king's spouses and concubines come next. Finally the king appears, "standing on an elephant, and holding the precious sword in his hand." At times the king makes a less dramatic appearance, in which case, "he uses only a golden palanquin, carried by four girls from the palace."

Chiu Ta-Kuan's chronicles describe the glory of the Angkor Court, reflecting the "historical" bas-relief of Angkor Vat. At a time when the Khmer monarchy's power was diminishing, although losing none of its splendour, the Chinese traveller's testimony is invaluable, as he brings to life a city which would be abandoned by its sovereigns some one hundred years later.

1 Terrace of the "Leper king", far north,
god represented as a king in his palace,
(early 13th cent.)

2 Bayon, bas-relief of the eastern outer gallery, south side. A travelling family of Khmer peasants.

3 Bayon, bas-relief of the eastern outer gallery, south side. Cooking.

4 Bayon, bas-relief of the eastern outer gallery, south side. The market.

5 "Adorned One at prayer, Angkor Vat",
(National Museum of Phnom Penh),
lacquered wood and gilded.

CHAPTER VIII

ANGKOR, THE CAPITAL ABANDONED

1. The last kings of Angkor

Srindravarman came to power in 1295 following the, perhaps voluntary, abdication of his father-in-law, Jayavarman VIII. Cambodian epigraphy mentions two kings as succeeding him. In 1307, Srindravarman abdicated as well, to be replaced by a relative, by the name of Srindrayavarman. This latter remained in power until 1327, at which time Jayavarmadiparmesvara ascended to the throne. Very little information about these kings exists. Under their reigns, Shaivism remained the Court religion, as is attested by the inscriptions and the donations made to the Mangalartha temple by Srindrajayavarman. Theravada Buddhism continued to gain in importance, however, and, with it, developed a knowledge of Pali. The first inscription written in Pali dates back to 1309.

After the Sanskrit inscriptions come from Kapilapura which mention Jayavarmadiparmesvara, Sanskrit inscriptions fall silent. Cambodian history over the next centuries is confined to a number of chronicles written during the late 18th or early 19th century. The most ancient text is the fragment of a chronicle, dated 1796, translated into

Siamese, and offered by the King of Cambodia, Ang Eng, to the King of Thailand[45]. Another chronicle was written, at the beginning of the 19th century, by an upper dignitary, Oknha Nong, by order of King Ang Chan. This last text was translated by Doudart de Lagrée, and published by Francis Garnier. The chronology of these two texts, unfortunately, does not coincide. They also differ from a third version which was used by Moura. In order to trace Angkoran history at that period, however, there do exist foreign sources of documentation, notably Chinese, Thai, Vietnamese, Portuguese and Spanish[46].

We do not know the ties which linked Jayavarmadiparmesvara with Nirvanapada (whose khmerized name is Nirpean Bat), the first king cited by the chronicles. According to tradition, Nirvanapada was the son of the gardener who committed regicide, Neay Trasak Phaem, the "Chief of the sweet cucumbers".

A famous Cambodian legend recounts that a gardener, Trasak Paem, was cultivating his garden of succulent sweet cucumbers. The ruling king, who was extremely partial to these fruits, ordered the gardener to save his entire harvest for him and, in order that he not be robbed of a single cucumber, he gave the gardener a spear, with the order to kill all thieves who entered the garden. One night, overcome by a craving, the king slipped into the garden. Woe befell him. Trasak Phaem did not recognize him, so killed him. The king left behind only a daughter. The task of naming a successor fell to the royal elephant. The animal stopped in front of Trasak Phaem, and paid him homage. The gardener married the dead king's daughter, a custom which legitimized usurpers.

He was able to impose his authority on the most

powerful men of the kingdom, who had proved recalci-
trant. His son, Nirvanapada, succeeded him; many texts
place this ascension in 1346. This king, and his first successors, lived in Angkor.

It is difficult to ascertain the exact date upon which the
monarchy abandoned Angkor in order to settle in the
Mekong plain, under pressure of the Thai invasions. If
Nong[47] chronology is to be believed, the Thai king,
Ramadhipati, who founded the Ayudhya kingdom, seized
Angkor in 1353, under the reign of Nirvanapada's son. A
succession of Siamese princes held the Cambodian throne
but, around 1358, according to Nong, a Khmer prince took
back Angkor and was crowned king under the name of
Suryavamsa Rajadhiraja.

From this date forth, the state of war be- tween the
Khmer and the Thais was relatively permanent. Toward
1370, another Thai attack against Cambodia brought about
the fall of Angkor, yet again, the death of the ruling king
and the placing of a Siamese king on the Khmer throne.
According to Nong chronology, it is thus that the
Cambodian prince Chau Ponhea Yat put the Siamese king
to death and reclaimed power. Having been crowned after
twelve years of a rule, he decided to leave Angkor and to
establish his capital in the Mekong plain, first at Basan, in
the region of Srei Santhor, then in Phnom Penh. The chronicle reported by Moura places this event at a much later
date, and places Ponhea Yat's advent, and the abandonment of Angkor after its siege by King Ayudhya Paramaraja
II, in 1431. An American historian, M. O.W. Wolters[48],
based on a new interpretation of Chinese and Khmer

sources, believes that, following the invasion of 1370, the Cambodian king had already retreated to Basan, but that his successor returned to reside in Angkor. It appears certain that the ancient capital was deserted by the monarchs several times, before being abandoned definitively.

Based on what we now know, it is very difficult to retrace the sequence of events in Angkor in the 15th century. The total desertion of the capital was no doubt due to the Thai invasion of 1431. J. Boisselier believes that, at that time, the city was pillaged and Paramaraja II captured the divinities as well as all of the royal attributes, "especially those which resided at Rajyasri, removed no doubt, through breaches in the northern and southern parts of the enclosure" of Neak Pean[49]. He adds that,

"In obliging the attributes and the guarantees of royalty to change masters, in making them take their place in Ayu-dhya, Paramaraja II thought he had captured the power of the Shakravartin, from which his dynasty would benefit in that it would henceforth be thought to possess the power which Jayavarman VII had concentrated in Angkor."

The city appears to have been completely deserted and re-become forest, when the kings returned, once again, during the second half of the 16th century.

2. Renaissance during the 16th century

In 1528, King Ang Chan, after having vanquished a usurper, founded a new capital, Lovek, to the south of the Tonle Sap, halfway between Phnom Penh and the Great

Lake. Having fought off the Thais, he gained a certain power. It was he who rediscovered the city of Yashodharapura, abandoned for more than a century. Our knowledge of this rediscovery comes from a Portuguese chronicler by the name of Diego do Couto:

"Toward the year 1550 or 1551, as the king of Cambodia was going on an elephant hunt in the densest forests of all the kingdom; these (people) in battling with the bush, came upon imposing structures which had been overgrown on the inside by the prolific foliage which they were not able to cut through, in order that they might enter. When the king heard of this, he went to that place and, seeing the height and breadth of the outer walls, also desired see the inside, straight-away ordered that all the plants be cut and burned. He remained there,.on the banks of a beautiful river, during which time five or six thousand men toiled to complete the task... Once all had been carefully cleaned, the King went inside and, having explored the entire building, was struck with admiration for the scope of the constructions. And it was for this reason that he decided immediately to bring his Court there, as not only was the city of a great splendour by its ordinance, but also was it one of the best in the world as that region is extremely pleasant...[50]"

If Angkor Thom had been completely forgotten, such was not the case of Angkor Vat where, in 1546, the king had given orders to sculpt bas-reliefs in the north-east quadrant of the third enclosure. In fact, the two panels in this gallery had been, at the most, partly sketched out at the time of Suryavarman II[51]. G. Coedès translated the inscriptions relating to the start and finish of these works. The bas-reliefs were completed in 1566, the year of Ang Chan's death, according to Nong chronology. It illustrates Vishnuist myths. Even if many of the background figures were executed with an unbearable mediocrity, the images of the gods reveal a technique which is far superior, certain among them being extremely beautiful.

Paramaraja, son of and successor to Ang Chan I, settled in Kompong Krassang, in the Angkor region, in order to oversee military operations against Thailand. It is difficult to ascertain whether the king set up permanent residence in Angkor, although it is certain that his son, Satha I, who became king in 1576, settled in and repopulated the ancient capital for a time. F. Joao dos Santos speaks of this king's installation, "they traced paths toward the city, where the King of Camboja came with his Court, and where he now lives[52]". Portuguese and Spanish missionaries spent time in Angkor, and several chroniclers wrote descriptions of the city.

Traces of this re-occupation can be found in Angkor Thom. At monument number 486 and at Prah Pithu X, fragments of sculpture have been dated at the 16th century. At the northern end of the Elephants' Terrace, certain modifications and certain sculptures also date back to this time. At Angkor Vat, in an inscription dated 1577, the Queen Mother of Satha tells of her joy upon seeing completed her son's restoration of Angkor Vat, which she calls the Brah Bisnulok, or "The Holy World of Vishnu". In a lengthy inscription, dated 1579, ordered by the king himself, it is said that the sovereign, "restored the walls of the enclosure of Brah Bisnulok, stone by stone, refitted the roof with its nine-point arrow, which he embellished by covering it with gold.[53]"

Ceremonies also took place in the temple. This same

inscription recounts the rites performed at the birth and naming of one of Satha's sons: "Twelve days after (the birth), on a Sunday, were reunited H.M. the Queen, the Rajaguru, the Astrologer and the Brahminic professors, for the celebration of the naming ceremony. H.M. deigned to confer on her royal child the beneficial name of Brah Paramarajadhiraj."

After that, the newborn was carried to Brah Bisnoluk, meeting place of the guardian divinities and ancestors, where he was presented as Buddha's disciple. This 16th century account is of a royal ceremony, celebrated in accordance with a Brahminic rite for a Buddhist monarch, which can be witnessed to this day in the Court of Phnom Penh.

Angkor unfurled its royal splendour, once again, for a few decades. It appears, however, that the city had a religious value, above all. Lovek, where the sovereign settled some years later, probably remained the administrative centre. In fact, Satha was in Lovek when King Ayudhya, Naresvra, attacked Cambodia, after having triumphed in Burma. The Thais marched on Lovek, which fell in January 1594.

The siege of Lovek was a disaster from which the Khmer were incapable of recovering. While the king was dying in Laos, where he had taken refuge, his son languished in Srei Santhor, and the bush once again took over Angkor Thom. Religious life never ceased at Angkor Vat, however, where Buddha continued to receive homage from the devout, and where two monasteries were founded inside the walls.

3. Angkor during the seventeenth and eighteenth centuries

The capital was never to return to Angkor; the kings would reside in Srei Santhor, then in Oudong, near Lovek. The sovereigns would return to Angkor Vat on pilgrimages, however. The chronicles mention some of the kings' sojourns in Angkor. Moura's version tells of King Chau Ponhea Tho's tragic love story at Angkor Vat.

While the young king had worn the monk's habit for a number of months, his uncle, who was acting as regent, took his fiancée, princess Ang Vodey, from him and married her. In 1630, during a trip to the Court of Angkor, the king met Ang Vodey and had a secret meeting with her on the stairs of the outer terrace of Angkor Vat. The romance was to end tragically, however, as the two lovers fled but were later captured and put to death.

Another king, Chau Ponhea Chan, stayed several times in Angkor. He was travelling for pleasure when the Spanish came from Manila to meet him; in order to accomplish their mission, the foreigners were obliged to go to Angkor. After Chau Ponhea Chan's death in 1658, however, the chronicles make no more mention of royal sojourns in Angkor, which had apparently been deserted by the kings until modern times.

The kings no longer went to Angkor, although the people continued to make pilgrimages there.

There are numerous inscriptions which bear witness to the Cambodians' attachment to the old temple. These texts, which are generally engraved on pillars, were often commissioned by wealthy people or ministers who, in aging, hoped to acquire merit through performing a pious deed. The most touching are the accounts of donations and pilgrimages cut into the stone on the request of a group of commoners come from many villages. Hence, we learn that a few laymen, "men and women who were pure of heart", came in 1630 with an offering of five statues of Buddha. Sometimes, pilgrimages were made to Angkor Vat when visiting relatives who lived in the regions.

The pilgrims often gave statues of Buddha to the temple. These donations were sometimes quite considerable. In 1684, a high religious dignitary declared that he had erected, "a hundred gold and silver Buddhas, 34 new stone Buddhas and other statues; a total of 214 statues of Buddha[55]". Only the stone and wooden images have survived to this day. They were deposited in Angkor Vat's Central Sanctuary in the galleries and in the southern part of the Cruciform Courtyard, a place which was called the Prah Pean or "Thousand Saints (Buddha)". The wooden statues are the most beautiful of all. Certain figures are of Buddha clad in austere monastic dress; others represent the Joyous One covered in royal finery, crowned with a tiara, wearing his monk's habit, necklaces, bracelets and belts. These statues received a gold coating, applied under two coats of red and black lacquer. In fact, according to Buddhist texts, Buddha's complexion had a golden tint. Representations of people kneeling in a stance of veneration were also stored at Angkor Vat. The most magnificent of all the surviving statues is, without a doubt, the "Adorned One at prayer, Angkor Vat" which is housed in the National Museum of Phnom Penh. This perfectly elegant image, deep in meditation, expresses an exquisite tenderness.

It is a pity that certain images were damaged by their long stay in the humid, and somewhat decayed, galleries; at the beginning of the 18th century, a minister had complained of this decay, and worked to restore a number of damaged statues. In the grand inscription at Angkor Vat, he tells of the state in which he found these long-standing images:

"Next I repaired and restored the holy statues (of Buddha), which were broken into dispersed and missing pieces, broken at the neck, the head rolling, the feet in fragments, the arms scattered. Making a concerted effort to find them, to assemble them, to glue them back together, I restored them, re-guilded them, and returned them to their original state of beauty."

The consecration of statues was often accompanied by other offerings: silver or copper platters, banners, canopies and perfume. There is also mention of offerings consisting of food, clothing and straw mats for the monks who lived in the two monasteries which were built inside the walls of Angkor Vat. It sometimes occurred that the offerings were made by the family of a novice upon his arrival at the monastery.

While all urban life had long since disappeared from Angkor Thom, Angkor Vat remained the epitome of a venerated sanctuary, the place of predilection for the kingdom's guardian divinities and, from its summit, rose the sanctuary which is now dedicated to Buddha.

CONCLUSION

ANGKOR LIBERATED FROM THE FOREST

Much has been said about the discovery of Angkor at the end of the 19th century. In reality, Angkor had never slumbered in total desertion. In the Far-East, Angkor was never forgotten. At the beginning of the 17th century, a Japanese pilgrim came to Cambodia and drew a plan of Angkor Vat, a copy of which was made in 1715. A text by P. Chevreul, who travelled to Cambodia in 1768, bore witness to Angkor Vat's renown throughout South-East Asia, "known to all the gentiles of five or six great Kingdoms, as is Rome among the Christians". In the West, however, despite the numerous missionaries' testimonies, the ancient Cambodian capital remained practically unknown. It is true that the missionaries' accounts were not published, being housed in archives for the most part.

Credit for the first published description of Angkor is due to P. Bouilleveaux, in 1858. This account made many aware of the existence of the abandoned city, although its beauty seems to have totally escaped that author's eye. Angkor was revealed to the West a few years later by a naturalist, Mohout, who had been overwhelmed by the splendour of the ruins. Mohout died a short time after his stay in Angkor, in 1860, but his notes were published in a widely distributed magazine, "Le Tour du Monde". Soon, missions of explorers and scientific researchers applied themselves to the study of the ancient Khmer capital. Doudart de Lagrée made three trips to Angkor between 1863 and 1867; on his third voyage, he was accompanied by F. Garnier and L. Delaporte. In 1863, a German traveller, Bastian, drew the scholars' attention to the

Cambodian inscriptions, which particularly interested the Dutch epigraphist, Kern. Other study missions were undertaken by Pavie, Fournereau, General de Beylié and Aymonier. The creation of a Permanent Mission to Indochina, in 1898, soon to be known as the Ecole Française d'Extrême Orient (French Far East School), marked a turning point in the discovery of the ancient Khmer kingdom. Following a Franco-Siamese treaty in 1907, which rendered unto Cambodia the ruins of its ancient capital, the Commission of the Angkor Monuments was founded. It would be impossible to enumerate, here, all of the searchers and scholars who dedicated a part of their life to the restoration and study of Angkor. In this small work, we were able, however, to cite quite a number of them.

The first challenge was to liberate the monuments from the forest's clutches, sometimes half-buried in the earth and masses of fallen rock. Only Angkor Vat was accessible as it had remained a holy site, although its temple had decayed; the testimony of the devotee who restored the statues, in 1701, proves that no upkeep was performed. In 1908, the first preservationist, J. Commaille, began to extract the Great Square of Angkor Thom from its surroundings. After his death, his successor, H. Marchal, cleared away everything which had buried the Terraces. In 1919, work began on the temples outside the city.

It was not enough to liberate the monuments. They had to be restored and only very rudimentary methods were available. Hence, Bayon, which was studied for the first time by Dufour and Carpeaux between 1901 and 1904, was cleared between 1911 and 1913. Its restoration, undertaken by G. Trouvé in 1933, was continued by M. Glaize from 1939 to 1946. A recent study was done at Bayon on the means of protecting stones from rampant lichen. After 1930, a well established technique, that of anastylosis, which consists of restoring monuments with the materials found on site, was put into practice. H. Marchal had begun to exploit this procedure in 1931 for the reconstruction of Banteay Srei. M. Glaize applied it to the re-erection of Banteay Samre and Neak Pean. The acquisition of modern material made possible subsequent reconstruction projects such as the one of Baphuon, which was headed by P. Groselier. When war broke out in 1970, work continued nevertheless.

The epigraphists, the historians and archeologists pursued their research on Angkoran history. Hence, the art history studies of P. Stern, the aerial searches of V. Golubev and the epigraphic works of G. Coedès allowed for the discovery of the first site of Yashodharapura, and for the attribution of Bayon and Angkor Thom to Jayavarman VII. J. Filliozat studied the Khmer monuments within the context of Indian monuments and writings. J. Boisselier dedicated his research to the study of iconography and the symbolism contained in the monuments.

Angkor has been universally known for some time; votive royal ceremonies once again take place at Angkor Vat. In fact, the Great Square of Angkor Thom was the site chosen by Prince Sihanouk, in 1968, to trace the first furrow which marked the beginning of the growing season. At that time, in order to celebrate the Khmer New Year in April, an enormous throng of people, some of whom came from afar, stayed in Angkor for a few days and discovered the episodes of the Ramayana and the life of Buddha on the temple walls. Faithful to the past, villagers and city dwellers alike meditated for a few moments in Angkor Vat or Prah Prean's Central Sanctuary, before the images of Buddha veiled by the sweet smoke of thousands of sticks of incense.

Notes

1 J. Filliozat, Le symbolisme du monument du Phonm Bakheng, B.E.F.E.O., XLIX, p. 527

2 According to M.CL. Jacques, Etudes d'épigraphie cambodgienne, B.E.F.E.O., LVIII, Paris, p. 166

3 As in all Khmer inscriptions, the texts sculpted in the piers of Prasat Kravan give the dates in Indian eras, i.e. saka (78 AD).

4 Siva

5 M.A. Le Bonheur noted that the placement of these sanctuaries recalls certain layouts of the Wat Phu temple.

6 Mahayana, "Great means of progress toward salvation". A doctrine which was developed through speculations on the nature of Buddha and the Bodhisatva, it was adopted first in northern India, Tibet, China, Japan and Vietnam.

7 According to custom, the sanctuaries of a temple are always numbered successively, beginning with the central sanctuary, not starting at the temple's entrance.

8 J. Boisselier, professorial course at the Sorbonne, in February, 1971, and in Il Sud Est Asiatico, p. 197 and 132, note 28; and L.P. Briggs, The Ancient Khmer Empire, p. 140

9 G. Coedès, Inscriptions du Cambodge, Vol. V, p. 229

11 Dharma, order, law

12 Vishnu, resting on the ocean between cosmic epochs

13 G. Coedès, La stèle de Prah Khan, B.E.F.E.À., XL I, Hanoi, 1941, p. 285

14 Angkor Vat is not the only monument to have a well beneath its main sanctuary. IA well was also discovered in the Baksei Chamkrong pyramid which leads to a small underground chamber. Earlier still, probably around the 8th century, a small room was built beneath the central sanctuary of Ak Yom.

15 It must also be noted that west is also the cardinal point of Vishnu.

16 G. Coedès, Pour mieux comprendre Angkor, Paris, 2nd edition, 1947

17 J. Filliozat, Kailasaparampara, in Felicitation volumes of South-East Asian Studies to H.H. Prince Dhaninivat, Siam Society of Bangkok, 1965, p. 245

18 Chiu Ta-Kuan, Mémoires sur les coutumes du Cambodge, translated and annotated by Paul Pelliot, B.E.F.E.O., vol. II, Hanoir, 1902

19 J. Filliozat, Le temple de Hari dans le Harivarsha, Arts asiatiques, vol. VIII, sect. 3, 1961, p. 195

20 Jean Boisselier, La royauté khmère dans la seconde moitié du XII siècle - Les prédécesseurs de Jayavarman VII. Comm. Société Asiatique, June 3, 1963. See Prof. C. Caillat, Felicitations, vol. pub. Indologica

Tauinensia, vol. XIV, 1987-88, pp. 117-143

21 Ravana, Rama's enemy whose wife he had kidnapped, is a demoniac character, king of Lanka (Ceylan). The battle between Rama and Ravana forms the central plot of the Ramayana.

22 Yama, god of death, his residence is in the south.

23 G. Coedès, Inscriptions du Cambodge, Vol. II, p. 177

24 The Chinese designated Cambodia under the name of Chen-La, a name already attributed to the pre-Angkoran ancestor of Cambodia.

25 Ma Touan-lin, méridionaux, transl. Hervey de Saint-Denys. p. 557

26 The essential documents which allow us to retrace Jayavarman VII's career were published by G. Coedès. They are: La stèle de Prah Khan (B.E.F.E.O., XLI, p.288); La stèle de Prah Khan (B.E.F.E.O., VI, p.75) and La grande stèle du Phiméanakas, Inscriptions du Cambodge II, p. 161

27 M.J. Boisellier notes that, after the epigraphic references, the representations of the Khmer against the Chams recalls the battle of the gods against the asura. Ref. Il Sud-est asiatico, p. 220

28 Panini was the most eminent of Sanskrit grammarians. He was born in Gandhara, before the birth of Christ. He is presented as a model for all scholars.

29 P. Mus, Une révolution politico-religieuse, la catastrophe de 1177 à Angkor, Musée Guimet, Public conference held on January 12, 1969.

30 Lokesvara is a bodhisattva, a being who is ready to be Awakened, to become a Buddha, but who puts off his entry into Nirvana in order to save other beings, "not only from incarnations, but also from materiel dangers". He is called either Lokesvara, the "Lord of the worlds", or, the "Lord who looks down from on high", out of compassion.

31 L. Finot and V. Golubev, Le symbolisme de Neak Pean, B.E.F.E.O., XXIII, 1923, p. 401

32 J. Boisselier, Pouvoir royal et symbolisme architectural, Neak Pean et son importance pour la royauté angkorienne, A. As, vol. XXI, 1970, p. 91

33 M. Glaize, Les monuments du Groupe D'Angkor, 4th ed., Paris, Adrien Maisonneuve, 1993, p. 212, par. 71-74

34 G. Coedès, Les hôpitaux de Jayavarman VII, B.E.F.E.O., XL, 1940, p. 344; G. Coedès, Les gîtes d'étapes, B.E.F.B.O., XL, 1940, p. 347.

35 J. Boisselier, Il Sud Est Asiatico, pp. 217-218.
According to him, the naga and the divinities of the roadway represent the divine beings which Indra had placed at the entrance to the city of the gods, after his victory over the asura.

36 P. Mus, Le symbolisme d'Angkor Thom, CR., Académie des Inscriptions et Belles-Lettres, 1936, p. 57

37 J. Boisselier, Il Sud Est Asiatico, p. 220.

38 The garuda were mythical creatures, part human, part bird. They appear in both Buddhist and Brahmic iconography. Garuda is Vishnu's

mount.
39 J. Boisselier, Pouvoir royal et symbolisme architectural... p. 102
40 Mahayana, see p. 31
41 Theravada, doctrine of the "ancients". Based on primitive Buddhism, this doctrine was developed in Ceylon.
42 Chiu Ta-Kuan, Mémoires sur les coutumes du Cambodge, translated and annotated by Paul Peliot B.E.F.E.O. , vol. II, 1902, p. 54
43 Translation by Paul Pelliot, op. cit.
44 Greeting, joined hands raised to the brow.
45 G. Coedès Classification of Cambodian historic documents, housed in the library of the Ecole Française d'Extrême Orient (French Far East School), B.E.F.E.O., XVIII, 1918, p. 15
46 Mak Phœun, Chroniques royales du Cambodge, E.F.E.O., Paris, 1994
47 Errors in interpretation may occur due to the fact that, in the chronicles, dates are fixed according to 12 year cycles, each of which bears an animal's name.
48 O.W. Wolters, The Khmer King at Basan (1371-1373) and the restoration of the Cambodian chronology during the fourteenth and fifteenth centuries, Asia Major, n.s., vol. XII, part I, 1966, p. 44
49 Ref. supra, p. 88
50 B.-Ph. Grosselier, Angkor et le Cambodge au XIVe siècle d'après les sources portugaises et espagnoles, Paris, 1958, p. 69
51 G. Coedès, La date d'exécution des deux bas-eliefs tardifs d'Angkor Vat, published with a note by J. Boisselier, Note sur les bas-reliefs tardifs d'Angkor Vat, Journal asiatique, 1962, p. 237
52 B.-Ph. Grosselier, Angkor et le Cambodge..., p. 79
53 Saveros Lewitz, Textes en khmer moyen, B.E.F.E.O., LVII, 1970, p. 113
12 These texts are quoted by E. Aymonier in Le Cambodge, vol. III, Paris, 1904, p. 282

LIST OF KINGS
WHO RULED IN ANGKOR

Yashovarman I (889 - ca 910), posthumous name:
Paramasivapada
Harshavarman I (ca 910-922), posthumous name:
Rudraloka
Ishanavarman (922-928), posthumous name:
Paramarudraloka

King's residence in Koh Kher, 928-944

Rajendravarman II (944-968), posthumous name:
Shivaloka
Jayavarman V (968-1001), posthumous name:
Paramaviraloka
Udayadityavarman I (1001-1002)
Jayaviravarman (1002- ca 1006)
Suryavarman I (1002-1050), posthumous name:
Paramanirvanapada
Udayadityavarman II (1050-1066)
Harshavarman III (1066-1080) (?), posthumous name:
Sadasivapada
Jayavarman VI (1080-1107), posthumous name:
Paramakaivalyapada
Dharanindravarman I (1107-1113), posthumous name:
Paramanishkalapada
Suryavarman II (1113- ca 1145), posthumous name:
Paramavishuloka
Yashovarman II (?-1165)
Tribhuvanadityavarman (1165-1177)

Cham occupation

Jayavarman VII (1181-1218) (?), posthumous name:
Paramasaugatapada
Indravarman II (1218 (?) - 1243)
Jayavaraman VIII (1243-1295), posthumous name:
Paramesvarapada
Srindravarman (1295-1307)
Srindrajayavarman (1307-1327)
Jayavarmadiparamesvara (1327-?)

First king of the chronicles:
Nirvanapada, mid-14th century
Abandonment of Angkor under the reign of Chau Ponhea
Yat, end of the 14th or beginning of the 15th century.
Discovery of Angkor Thom in 1550-1551

SUMMARY BIBLIOGRAPHY

BHATTACHARYA, K. *Les religions brahmaniques dans l'ancien Cambodge, based on the epigraphy and iconography*, Paris, E.F.E.O. (French Far East School), vol. XLIX, 1961

BOISSELIER, J., *La statuaire khmère et son évolution*, Hanoi, E.F.E.O., vol. XXXVII, 2 vol., 1955

BOISSELIER, J., *Tendances de l'art khmèr*, Annals of the Musée Guimet, Paris, P.U.F., 1956

BOISSELIER, J., *South-East Asia, vol. I: Le Cambodge, Manuels d'Archéologie d'Extême-Orient collection*, Paris, Picard, 1966

BOISSELIER, J., *Note sur l'art du bronze dans l'ancien Cambodge*, Artibus, Asie, Ascona, 1967

BOISSELIER, J., *Il Sud-est Asiatico,* in Storia Universale dell'arte U.T.E.T., Torino, 1986

BRIGGS, L.P., *The Ancient Khmer Empire*, Philadelphia, American Philosophical Society, 1951

COEDES, G., *Pour mieux comprendre Angkor*, Paris, 2nd ed., 1947

COEDES, G., *Les Etats hinouisés d'Indochine et d'Indonésie*, "Histoire du Monde" collection, vol. VIII, 2, Paris, de Boccard, 1948

COEDES, G., *Les peuples de la péninsule Indochinoise,* "Sigma" collection, vol. 2, Paris, 1962

COEDES, G., L., *Inscriptions du Cambodge, "Textes et Documents de l'Indochine" collection, III,* 8 vols, Hanoi, then Paris, E.F.E.O., 1937-1966

CORAL-REMUSAT, G. de, *L'art khmèr, les grandes étapes de son évolution,* Paris, Editions d'Art et d'Histoire, 2nd ed., 1951

DAGES, B., *Angkor, la forêt de pierre,* Découverte-Gallimard collection, Paris, Gallimard, 1969

DAUPHIN-MENIER, A., *Histoire du Cambodge,* "Que-sais-je" collection, Paris, P.U.F., 1961

FINOT, L., GOLUBEV, V., and COEDES, G., *Le temple d'Angkor Vat,* Archeological memoirs of the Ecole Française d'Extrême Orient, II, 7 vols, Paris, Van Oest, 1929-1932

GITEAU, M., *Les Khmers, sculptures khmères, reflets de la civilisation d'Angkor,* Fribourg, Office du Livre, 2nd ed., 1972

GITEAU, M., *Iconographie du Cambodge Post-angkorien,* Paris, E.F.E.O., vol. C, 1975

GITEAU, M., *Regards sur Angkor,* Chapître Douze Ed., Pais, 1994

GLAIZE, M., *Les monuments d'Angkor,* Guide, Paris, A. Maisonneuve, 4th ed., 1993

TABLE OF CONTENTS

Imprimé en France
Janvier 1998
Imp. Durand
9, rue du Maréchal-Leclerc
BP 69 - 28600 Luisant
02 37 24 48 00